"This book could save your church from needless ~~~~~~ ~~~ ~~~~~~~. Listen and learn from it!"
Rick Warren
Senior Pastor, Saddleback Church, Lake Forest, California

"Larry writes like a wise caring mentor, sharing his profoundly simple proven approach to getting your team to work together without splits, shouting matches or a "range war board." If you are a pastor, consider re-reading this book once a year for the rest of your life."
Bobb Biehl
President, Masterplanning Group International

"…Often I wish your book *The Unity Factor* was back in print so I could recommend it to pastors. It's a great book."
John Maxwell
Founder The INJOY Group

"North Coast Church is one of the healthiest congregations I know. One of the big reasons is the solid leadership of its lead pastor, Larry Osborne. *The Unity Factor* shares excellent principles and insights from the North Coast team that have guided this church for over 20 years. …unlike a lot of books, this one gets better with age."
Dave Travis
Vice President: The Leadership Network

"Larry Osborne's message will save a pastor years of frustration with his veteran insights. He's 'been there and done that' with leaders. He has helped me more than once to clarify my leadership strategy. His life and church is living proof he knows what he's talking about!"
Steve Sjogren
Founding Pastor, Vineyard Community Church, Cincinnati, Ohio

"I have encouraged students, pastors and other church leaders by the hundreds to own this pithy and powerful volume. . . People thank me across the country for the meaningful ministry it has had in melting minds and egos in the task of making Christ the Lord of our churches."
Warren Benson
Sr. Professor of Christian Education & Leadership, Southern Baptist
Theological Seminary, Louisville, Kentucky

"I loved *The Unity Factor* when I first read it several years ago. Few books become more relevant as they age. But Larry's wisdom on leadership is more helpful to me now than ever. It's clarity and simplicity cut through the glut of contemporary punditry. My hope is that a fresh generation of readers will find
new direction in this updated version."
Bill Hull
Pastor & Writer, Cypress, California

"Too many leaders serve on their church board with the bad taste of disunity in their mouth. *The Unity Factor* is like a box of powerful spiritual breath mints. No other leadership book has sweetened the atmosphere of our board meetings like this one. Get it. Get close. And get moving together."
Dave Miller
Senior Pastor, The Church at Rocky Peak, Chatsworth, California

"One of the critical issues in a healthy church is a close working relationship between boards and pastors. *The Unity Factor* is a wonderful guide and starting point for a discussion as to how this relationship can be negotiated for maximum ministry effectiveness and minimum friction. I recommend it highly as a key resource for church leadership boards."

William J. Hamel
President, Evangelical Free Church of America

"For every pastor and church leader who struggles with people issues, The Unity Factor, reminds us that we are on the same team and gives great examples on how we can work together and create healthy churches. I especially appreciated Dr. Osborne's ability to tear down the adversarial attitudes between pastors, lay leaders and board members. Thank you for showing us (pastors) that working with a board can be enjoyable and beneficial and doesn't have to be a miserable and adversarial experience."

Rick Olmstead
Pastor, Vineyard Church of Fort Collins

"The Unity Factor is biblical, practical and highly effective. I use it as a refresher course for our Elder Leadership Team on a regular basis. Osborne understands what brings out the best in church leaders. This book works!"

Steve Goold
Pastor Crystal Evangelical Free Church, New Hope, Minnesota

"Larry Osborne has written a great book on leadership with the focus on the proper functioning of a governing board. His section on 'Let Squeaky Wheels Squeak' is worth the price of the book."

Michael Andrus
Pastor, First Evangelical Free Church of Saint Louis, Manchester, Missouri

"...Larry Osborne has made an outstanding contribution in his very readable, practical, and biblically-sound book, The Unity Factor, which I found to be of immense help, not only for church boards, but also for the boards of non-profit organizations. This is not some theoretical abstract, but full of insight and wisdom which come tested from the arena of practical experience."

Clyde Cook
President, Biola University, La Mirada, California

"...I've worked with countless competent pastors whose ministries would have been longer and much more fruitful if they had understood even a few of the principles in Larry's book. The chapters on 'What The Board Needs To Know' are worth the price of the book. The Unity Factor comes from the heart of a brother who is a faithful student of God's Word, a wise teacher and a experienced leader. Larry has given leaders a valuable gift and essential resource. I promise you that this is a book you will read more than once. In fact, you will turn to it again and again for simple, practical wisdom on how to lead with courage, clarity and compassion."

Gary Oliver
Executive Director, The Center for Marriage and Family Studies and LeaderCARE, John Brown University, author of Made Perfect In Weakness:
The Amazing Things God Can Do With Failure

"One of the amazing things that has gripped me with joy is that there is no difference between Larry Osborne the man and the content of The Unity Factor. He has participated in my leadership class for fourteen semesters. Without exception, the students feel his time to be the most important three hours of the semester."

Wallace Norling
Superintendent Emeritus Evangelical Free Church of America

"Larry Osborne comes out of the trenches of church leadership and shares insights that should be a 'must read' for every pastor and Christian leader. This material is among some of the best that I have read."

Thomas McDill
Title: Past President, Evangelical Free Church of America

THE
UNITY
FACTOR

Developing a Healthy
Church Leadership Team

Larry W. Osborne

4th Edition
Published by Owl's Nest
1132 North Melrose Drive
Vista, California 92083

THE UNITY FACTOR
4th Edition

© 1989 Larry W. Osborne

Published by OWL'S NEST

Cover Design – Mel Caines
Cover Photograph – Foto Giuseppe Ghedina – Corina

Library of Congress Cataloging-in-Publication Data

Osborne, Larry W., 1952-
The unity factor: developing a healthy church leadership team / Larry W. Osborne.

1. Church officers. 2. Church meetings. 3. Christian leadership.

ISBN-10: 0-9708186-1-0
ISBN-13: 978-0-9708186-1-4

Printed in the United States of America
1st Printing 1989
2nd Edition 1995
3rd Edition 2001
4th Edition 2006

To Mike, Paul, and the rest of the board:
Thanks for your patience, support, and love.

To my parents, Bill and Carolyn:
Thanks for providing your love, life wisdom and a
Godly model worth following.

CONTENTS

| INTRODUCTION

What causes you to feel discouraged in ministry?

Leadership Journal asked that question of its readers not long ago. Near the top of the list, identified by nearly 40 percent of the respondents, was this succinct answer: "Board meetings."

In a separate, earlier study, Leadership asked, "What topics would you be most interested in reading a book about?" A whopping two-thirds of the pastors surveyed said this: "How can we have shorter, better board meetings?"

In response, Leadership went to a pastor whose articles about working with the board have received high marks from our readers. We knew Larry Osborne would provide not wishful thinking but well-grounded, true-to-life approaches, ones that he's tested with his own board. In The Unity Factor, Larry draws on that experience to identify the roadblocks to a unified board and help us remove them.

The Leadership Library began with Well-Intentioned Dragons, a book that explored how to minister to problem people, those who rupture a church's unity. Now we're happy to announce The Leadership Library's culmination in The Unity Factor, which approaches the same question from a different angle: how to prevent disunity by developing a healthy and united church leadership team.

— Kevin A. Miller
Senior Associate Editor
Leadership Journal

ONE

THE MISSING INGREDIENT

When I arrived at the church, I was armed with books and ideas on growth, evangelism, and reaching the community. Unity was the last thing I was worried about. If you'd told me to slow down and focus on camaraderie and unity, I'd have chided you for your inward, even self-centered, approach to ministry. We had a world to conquer. But it soon became painfully obvious that we were never going to change the world out there when we couldn't get along in here.

I t's no secret that serving on the church board can be a tough assignment. I learned this early in life when my dad became a deacon. Often, late hours and acrimonious debates left him physically exhausted and emotionally spent. Like many lay leaders (over 80 percent according to one study), he found his stint on the board hurt, rather than helped, his spiritual growth.

But lay leaders aren't the only ones who find board meetings a harrowing experience. So do many pastors. The combination of marathon sessions and simmering conflict can make working with the board one of the least satisfying aspects of ministry.

No one wants it this way. For most of us there is a gnawing sense that this can hardly be what the Spirit had in mind when he sent out Paul and Barnabas to appoint elders. But if truth be known, it's not a new problem. From Miriam and Aaron's quarrel with Moses, to the Corinthian disputes, to Euodia and Syntyche's clash at Philippi, to last week's church split at First Community, God's leaders sometimes have had a hard time getting along.

Still, like most pastors, I was surprised when it happened at my church. I had thought I would be immune. I wasn't.

Six months into my first senior pastorate, I found myself embroiled in controversy. The church was losing old members as fast as we could bring in new ones. The board and I were having a hard time seeing eye to eye on anything. At night, I'd lie in bed and wonder what I'd do if they asked me to leave, or if the church split, or if a congregational meeting suddenly turned raucous.

Fortunately none of those things happened. With God's help, a once-divided board became a united leadership team. But it didn't happen overnight. Along the way, we had some important lessons to learn. None was more important than this: A unified leadership team doesn't just happen. It has to be a priority.

Why Worry about Unity?

That lesson didn't come naturally to me. When I arrived at the church, I was armed with books and ideas on growth, evangelism, and reaching the community. Unity was the last thing I was worried about. If you'd told me to slow down and focus on camaraderie and unity, I'd have chided you for your inward, even self-centered, approach to ministry. We had a world to conquer.

But it soon became painfully obvious that we never were going to change the world out there when we couldn't get along in here. So I set aside my other goals, and for the next two and a half years I made the development of a cohesive leadership team my number-one priority. Today, maintaining that unity remains at the top of my list, far ahead of church growth, evangelism, and every other worthy goal.

Why the change?

First, I've learned that *as the leadership board goes, so goes the rest of the church.* If we're at war in the board room, it doesn't matter how well things are going in the church at large. If the fighting doesn't stop, eventually there will be a coup d'etat or a resignation.

That's what happened to my friend Andy. As far as everyone in the congregation was concerned, things were going great. After five years of decline, the church was once again growing; the young people were returning; giving was at an all-time high.

But there were three families he could never please, all of whom were represented on the deacon board. Close friends of the previous pastor, and still in monthly contact with him, they took as a personal affront every change Andy made. If anyone in the church had a complaint or was unhappy, these board members were sure to hear about it and bring it up at the next board meeting.

The difference between the board's perspective of Andy's ministry and the congregation's perspective was amazing. Listening in on a board meeting, you'd have thought the church was on the edge of disaster. Sitting in a worship service, you'd have thought it was on the verge of explosive growth.

But no matter how much affirmation Andy received from the congregation, it was still the board to whom he reported. They set his salary, approved or vetoed his ideas, and controlled much of what he could and could not do. After a couple of years of battles with the board, Andy quit. The congregation was shocked, and the church nearly split.

Sadly, in conversations with fellow pastors, I've heard plenty of variations on Andy's story: a supportive congregation and a divided board. But there is one story I've yet to hear: a pastor bemoaning a divided congregation while at the same time singing the praises of a supportive and united board. It doesn't seem to happen. Why? Because as the board goes, so goes the rest of the church.

The second reason I've chosen to make unity a priority is that *without it, it's nearly impossible to sustain spiritual growth.*

As a pastor, it's my job to see that people are brought to spiritual maturity. I once thought that could be accomplished by putting together challenging sermons, forming discipleship groups, and helping people to identify and use their spiritual gifts. I still consider those important, but I now realize I was leaving out a vital first step: creating an environment conducive to spiritual growth. As a farmer needs to clear the land before planting his crop, I also need to clear out any conflict with the board before trying to plant and reap a spiritual harvest.

Jesus said strong things about forgiveness. When the board refuses to heed those words, we hardly can expect our church to be blessed with spiritual power. It's been my experience that when the board fights — whether in a civil war or a cold war — our people are more likely to grow in cynicism than in faith.

The third reason developing board unity remains at the top of my list is that it's fragile. Like love in a marriage, harmony in a board needs special attention or it will die.

I once took unity for granted. I assumed committed Christians who shared a common Lord and a common goal couldn't help but get along. But I badly underestimated the powerful forces at work to pull us apart. We came from diverse backgrounds, and most of us assumed our way was the best way. Add in our selfish sin nature, and you can see why unity was in such short supply.

Sadly, in every town in which I've served, at least one church experienced booming growth only later to collapse like a house of cards. Each time the problem has been the same: a dynamic ministry, great programs, lots of excitement, but an unstable, disunified leadership base.

I don't think it's an accident that Jesus predicted church growth but prayed for unity. If left unattended, or taken for granted, unity can disappear. All it takes is a few wrong people on the board, a passionate disagreement over how to handle a tough issue, or even a series of minor annoyances left to fester. One was certain, the other tenuous. That's why I've taken to heart Paul's advice in Ephesians 4:3: "Make every effort to keep the unity of the Spirit through the bond of peace."

Defining Unity

Deciding to make unity a priority is one thing. Figuring out what that means in practical terms is another.

In talking with pastors, I've come to the conclusion that for many of us, *unity* is a vague term. While we easily recognize its presence or absence, few of us have spelled out carefully its essential elements. Yet that's an all-important first step in developing a unified leadership team. Before we can hit the target, we have to know what we're aiming for.

When I realized that I had no idea what a unified board was supposed to look like, I began asking questions: Is there room for doctrinal disagreement? If so, how much? Can we have a split vote and still be unified, or does unity mean unanimity? How close are our relationships supposed to be?

Eventually, I settled on three irreducible components, things we must have in order to become a unified leadership team:

1. Doctrinal purity
2. Sincere and warm friendships
3. Philosophical purity (basic agreement on our priorities and methods).

By *doctrinal purity*, I mean agreement with our church's statement of faith, but I don't mean theological uniformity. Our leadership team contains charismatics and noncharismatics, and those pre-trib and post-trib. And we certainly don't all see eye to eye on the so-called lifestyle issues. Yet, we've been able to live and work together in harmony.

One reason our theological diversity has not destroyed our unity is that we've done more than just state what we believe; we've also made it clear what we *won't* fight over. In nearly every doctrinal fight I've witnessed, the debate has not raged over an issue spelled out in the doctrinal statement but over a peripheral concern. That's why, for the sake of unity, doctrinal purity needs to go beyond lockstep agreement with the statement of faith; it also needs to include agreement over what areas are nonessential, and therefore, allow for freedom of interpretation. Otherwise, sooner or later someone will try to add his favorite doctrine to the list of essentials, and when he does, he will wage war with those who disagree.

The second component, *sincere and warm friendships*, refers to a camaraderie built around genuine appreciation and respect for one another. It doesn't mean everyone has to be best friends. But it does mean that we get along well enough to avoid the miscommunication, stereotyping, and personality conflicts that can so easily dominate the discussion of tough issues.

Yet I've found that in many board settings, the members might as well be strangers. We may know one another's name and have a casual acquaintance, but that's about it. When I arrived at North Coast, one board member was going through serious psychological difficulties, and another's marriage was on the rocks. None of the rest of us knew about either problem. No wonder we found unity hard to come by.

Concentrating on friendship has paid rich dividends. It's made serving on the board an enjoyable experience. We no longer have a hard time getting good people to serve; they want to serve. The personality clashes and picky arguments that used to waste time in our meetings have disappeared. We've become more creative and willing to try new things. Most important, our old "watchdog mentality" (making sure no one got by with anything) has been replaced by a new spirit of cooperation and teamwork.

But developing sincere and warm friendships doesn't mean everyone hangs out together. Frankly, we don't spend that much time together outside of board meetings and church activities. We are not a tight clique. We are co-workers who've developed a mutual respect by applying the strategies you'll find in the following pages. In short, we've become friends.

The final component, *philosophical purity*, was by far the hardest to develop. In a volunteer organization like the church, it can take a long time to hammer out a consensus on priorities and ways of doing things. In our case, it was nearly four years before we were all headed the same direction.

Maintaining philosophical purity doesn't mean we all think alike. It's not a call for clones or even unanimity; there's plenty of room for disagreement. But if we are going to work together effectively, we have to be playing off the same sheet of music. Otherwise, we'll be like a small ensemble to which everyone brings his own favorite arrangement, and the resulting sounds will be chaos, not harmony.

For example, my friend Paul remembers two board members at his previous church. Don was older, stoic, and a defender of tradition. Rumor had it he wore a three-piece suit to bed. Rick was younger, emotional, and eager to try new things. More than once he came to church decked out in a Hawaiian shirt. They seldom saw eye-to-eye on anything, and their fundamental differences often spilled over into the board meeting. Yet, ironically, no matter what the issue, each defended his position with the argument: "This is the best way to reach people for Christ." Though they shared the same theology and the same bottom-line goals, they couldn't have been further apart when it came time to choose methods.

Most church fights aren't over theology or even ministry goals; they're over priorities and methodology. When Dave and Pat argue over how to spend money (whether to set it aside for a new building or use it to hire a youth pastor), they're arguing over priorities. When Kelly and Walt debate the merits of Bach and pipe organs versus guitars and drums, they're arguing over methods. Both want to worship the Lord; they just disagree over the best way to go about it.

Developing and nourishing a shared philosophy of ministry, then, is one of the most important things a pastor and board can do to maintain unity.

Finding Unity

A unified leadership team, though neither quick nor easy to build, is well worth the effort. As our board pulled together, so did a once-splintered congregation.

Not long ago I asked a new member who had been involved in many churches over the years why she and her husband had settled at North Coast.

"There were two reasons," she said. "First, we couldn't believe the lack of pressure to join. And second, we've never been in such a unified church. Usually, after you've been around for a while, when you get together in smaller groups, you hear people complaining about the board, the pastor, or the staff. We've never heard that. Maybe we don't hang around with the right people!"

On the one hand, her answer made my day. It reminded me of how far we'd come. But on the other hand, I found it discouraging, a reminder that in more churches than I want to admit, unity remains the missing ingredient.

The rest of this book focuses on many of the key lessons we learned (as well as the mistakes we made) while striving to put together a healthy and unified leadership team. Each of the three main sections deals with a different part of the process. The first, *Structure*, examines some of the common ways church boards are inadvertently structured for disunity and how we can remove those roadblocks. The next section, *Training*, looks at the positive impact training can have upon a board's unity, and shows how to put together a training program. The final section, *Communication*, explores practical strategies for defusing the land mines of change, evaluation, and negotiation. I pray these principles and strategies will help your board to become more unified and effective in your service for the Lord.

T W O

REMOVING THE ROADBLOCKS

*For the most part, our board members were good
and godly folks who sincerely wanted to know
and do God's will. Yet somehow we could hardly
make a decision without conflict. The problem?
We had unwittingly structured ourselves for
confrontation and division.*

I'll never forget one of my first board
meetings at North Coast. We had begun with prayer and
devotions. But while Jim tried hard to minister to our
spirits, hardly anyone listened. Most of the board
members leafed through the financial statements. A few
stared into space.

After a brief round of reports, we moved to the business at hand. I assumed we were in for a short meeting. The only items on the agenda were two purchases: a Communion tablecloth and tires for the church-owned pastor's car.

But the tablecloth brought forth a long and petty discussion. The tires sparked a full-scale debate. For half an hour, two men squared off over new tires versus retreads. When we finally settled it with a vote, the new tires won on a split decision.

And I didn't want or need the car in the first place.

What's Causing the Problem?

Most pastors can relate similar stories. With them, I've wondered, *What is it about board meetings that seems to bring out the worst in people? Why do so many church boards experience conflict?*

I once thought the problem was sin and pride. The way I saw it, church boards were notorious for fighting because so many board members were carnal. The solution was simple: Get people right with God, and conflict will cease.

But I've come to realize that sin and pride aren't always the key players. In fact, some of the most significant causes of conflict are sociological, not spiritual. For the most part, our board members were good and godly folks who sincerely wanted to know and do God's will. The problem was, we had unwittingly structured ourselves for confrontation and division. Our systems and traditions were sabotaging our unity.

Once I saw how these structural roadblocks were hindering our effectiveness and unity, I began to identify and remove as many of them as possible. The results were dramatic. Posturing and infighting began to be replaced by a spirit of teamwork and cooperation. And a board that was once unable to agreeably purchase tablecloths and tires learned to tackle successfully the truly significant issues of ministry.

Four of these roadblocks to board unity stand out as particularly common and damaging to a board's unity.

The Wrong Meeting Place

One of the most common and frequently overlooked roadblocks to unity is the location of our meetings. I'm convinced many church boards meet in the wrong place.

When I came to North Coast, we met for worship in a high-school cafeteria. We held our monthly board meetings in my office, a large refurbished garage. There, on the first Thursday of every month, I witnessed a mysterious transformation. What had earlier in the day been a place of study and prayer suddenly turned into a battleground of ideas and personalities. Members who had been warm and friendly on Sunday morning turned critical and petty on Thursday night. Folks who took copious notes of everything I said in a pulpit now questioned everything I said in a board meeting.

While the seating was uncomfortable, the lighting poor, and the room a little cold, I gave little thought to how our environment might be affecting these meetings. Then one day, in desperation after a particularly rough meeting, I suggested we hold our board meetings at my home. I figured the change in ambience couldn't hurt, and it might help.

As soon as we began meeting in my home, everyone relaxed their body language, terminology, and even dress. When dealing with tough issues, we were noticeably more cordial. When meetings were over, people began to stay and talk.

Why the sudden change? Because our change in environment brought about a change in our behavioral expectations. When we meet in an office or board room environment, we are surrounded by symbols of the corporate world, where confrontation and competition are expected. But when we meet in a home, the behavioral expectations are warmth, cooperation, and friendship.

Not every board has the luxury of meeting in a home. Some boards are too large, and some may not have an adequate home available. But nearly every board can find ways to increase the warmth and informality of its meeting place. Too often, we've settled for rooms that are cramped, uncomfortable, and poorly lit, or oversized, sterile, and fluorescent-lit. I know of one board that sits in rigid rows, with most members staring at the back of another's head. It comes as no surprise they seldom have a quality discussion.

There are times when a large conference table or traditional site works best — for example, when hammering out budget details, nominations, or long-range plans. But most church boards can greatly increase their harmony simply by meeting in the more intimate environment of a home. This switch paid the quickest dividends of any change we made.

Business at the Expense of Relationships

A second roadblock we had to overcome was our tendency to put business concerns above relational concerns. Like many lay leaders, most of our board members defined their role in terms of a task to be done. Building relationships was nice, but hardly necessary.

I opened one meeting with a series of get-acquainted questions. The next morning, over breakfast, our chairman informed me that elder meetings were not the proper time for such nonsense. "It's just too inefficient," he said. "We have plenty of other times and places for socializing."

This outlook — that meetings exist for business and business only — is one of the main reasons why prayer and devotions are often viewed as preliminaries to the "real meeting," and why few agendas include time for cultivating relationships.

I began to look for ways to emphasize relationships without making the board feel as if we were suddenly turning into an encounter group. The first step was scheduling an all-day retreat. We jammed into a van and headed south for an old resort hotel. As we traveled and ate meals, a new spirit of togetherness began to develop. We laughed as a die-hard union man and a top-level executive exchanged teasing barbs. We listened intently as one man explained the pressures he had been feeling at work. For most of us, it was the first time we had any idea he was considering a move. By the time we arrived home, we had experienced more laughter, kidding, and deep personal dialogue than in all our previous meetings combined.

We now get away at least twice a year. Along with building better relationships, these times produce our best brainstorming sessions and most insightful critiques of ministry, staff, and programs.

There are many other ways to emphasize relationships. Some boards eat together before each meeting. Others regularly schedule social events. A simple way to increase social interaction among board members is to schedule a refreshment break in the middle of meetings. Like many groups, we used to serve coffee and dessert at either the beginning or end of a meeting. But a few members always arrived just as the meetings began and left immediately after they were over. Rushing in and rushing out, they rarely shared in the casual conversations that cultivate friendship. Invariably, they were the very people who most needed to develop a closer rapport with the group. By placing our break in the middle of the meeting, I was able to insure that everyone participated in some face-to-face social time.

These are just some of the ways to overcome a roadblock that hinders the unity of many church boards: the tendency to focus on business and ignore relationships.

Infrequent Meetings

A third roadblock was our tendency to meet as infrequently as possible. The last thing most people want is another meeting. Our board members were no exception. Each summer, when vacation plans made it difficult for everyone to get together, someone would suggest skipping the next meeting. We were always quick to agree. As a result, we often met fewer than twelve times a year. While this may have been great for freeing up busy schedules, it played havoc with our board's unity. We simply weren't together often enough to develop into a cohesive leadership team.

Like most boards, we were, and are, a diverse group. To develop what Peter Drucker has called the "essential ingredient for teamwork: mutual respect,"[1] we needed to know each other well enough to have confidence in each other's ability to perform. This wasn't likely to happen when our goal was to meet as briefly and as infrequently as possible.

Most boardroom conflicts spring out of our different ways of viewing life. A corporate executive, self-employed contractor, middle manager, and school administrator will always see things differently. Their educational and professional backgrounds give them radically different points of reference. For instance, the man who argued for retreads on our church car was a long-time blue-collar worker. He and his wife enjoyed garage sales. The man who wanted the new tires was a former mayor; he was used to overseeing the expenditure of millions. I don't think he had bought anything secondhand in his life.

To help get such diverse people on the same page, I did something I never thought I would do: I scheduled an extra monthly board meeting. I did it to take advantage of a principle of group dynamics: Whenever a group of people increases the amount of their interaction with one another, there will be a corresponding increase in their regard and appreciation for one another.[2] We called this extra meeting a "shepherding meeting." I'll discuss it in more detail in chapter 7, but for now it's important to note that no votes or business decisions were allowed. We focused on prayer, team building, instruction in practical ministry, and seeking a common vision.

These meetings helped us to get on the same page. To keep them there, we made them a permanent fixture. Short-term meetings, seminars, or retreats can solidify a board, but the results of one-time events are usually short-lived, lasting at most until the makeup of the board changes. With regular shepherding meetings, the effects last, and we have an increasing backlog of shared experiences from which to draw.

The larger the board, the greater the benefit of these extra meetings. Larger boards, by nature, limit face-to-face encounters, which is one of the main reasons larger boards tend to experience more conflict. Yet in most cases, the larger a board gets, the more likely it is to schedule fewer (and longer) meetings in the hope of enabling everyone to attend. While this may cut down on absenteeism, it also undercuts unity. Unity depends on regular, close contact.

Constant Turnover

A final roadblock I'll mention is, ironically, often legislated by a church's constitution. It's a rotating board.

In the typical setup, members serve a three-year term. The terms are staggered, so that each year one-third of the members rotates off the board to be replaced by a new group. When a person completes a three-year term, he usually must wait at least a year before becoming eligible to serve again.

On the surface, this approach appears to have significant advantages. It guarantees a mix of new blood and experience. It cuts down on recruitment, since only one-third of the board has to be replaced each year. It assures continuity, since two thirds of the board have at least a year's experience. It also makes it difficult for a clique to monopolize power. However, for many pastors, the greatest advantage of this system is that it offers a gracious way to remove an ineffective or divisive board member. Just wait three years, and the member will be gone.

Despite these benefits, a rotating board can do more harm than good. Imagine a corporation that changed one-third of its leaders every ten to fifteen meetings. The lack of continuity would give rise to constant jockeying for position. Little work would get done. Then, just about the time the group started to jell, it would be time for another changing of the guard. But that is exactly what happens in most churches. The high rate of turnover makes developing and maintaining a cohesive team extremely difficult.

While I believe some turnover is good and even necessary, in most cases, one-third is too much. It means that 33 percent of the board lacks a corporate memory, and it makes it hard to build on past decisions. Old battles are likely to be refought year after year. Faced with complex decisions, new members often want to go back to square one, unable or unwilling to build on past decisions and discussions in which they had no part.

(It's important to note that some boards allow people to serve two terms in succession before asking them to take a sabbatical. That takes care of the high, 33-percent annual turnover rate.)

Although a rotating board can provide a painless way to remove painful people, let's not forget it forces out the good ones as well. Once a term is up, there is no way to keep a person on the board, even if that person is desperately needed. One church had its two best lay leaders rotate off the board soon after losing a senior pastor. For twelve months the church had neither a senior pastor nor a regular interim. During that time, it needed the leadership and wisdom of these two men. But they were shut out of the system, unable to use their God-given gifts and wisdom until they had waited out a forced sabbatical that no one wanted in the first place.

There are other ways to remove painful people from the board besides rotating them out of the system. (Perhaps the best way is to keep them off the board in the first place, which we will discuss in the next chapter.) But assume the damage has been done, and the painful member already has a position on the board. At the risk of sounding simplistic, I've found the best solutions to be prayer and/or honest confrontation. Neither is painless or easy, but both are rather biblical.

Instead of legislating constant turnover, we've set it up so board members are elected to one-year terms that can be renewed indefinitely. To insure that we don't become out of touch with, or unaccountable to, the congregation, the incumbents are treated just like new nominees. They have to be reelected individually each year. We use a simple yes/no ballot, and we ask everyone who casts a "no" vote for a nominee to write reasons for that vote next to the person's name. So far, we've never had a candidate rejected by the congregation, and I expect we never will, because our candidates are carefully screened. But we take every "no" vote seriously and review it with the board member involved.

Allowing board members to serve indefinitely hasn't resulted in an ingrown board. It's resulted in a stable board. Changing schedules and family and work situations naturally create turnover — more than enough to give a healthy combination of new blood and experience.

This system allows us to enjoy the advantages of a rotating board without committing ourselves to wholesale changes each year. It's given us the freedom to choose how many board members should be added or removed. And it's enabled us to avoid one of the more common roadblocks to unity: constant turnover.

Removing these four roadblocks radically changed our board. One incident stands out in my mind whenever I reflect upon the contrast.

A young father and I sat talking in my office. A change in his wife's work schedule and other commitments had made it impossible for him to serve on the board during the coming year.

As he told me his decision, his eyes began to fill with tears. I knew him well, but I had never seen him cry before. He wasn't the type. When he finally spoke, he said simply, "I'm going to miss the guys."

Though disappointed to lose him, I couldn't help myself; as soon as he left my office I let out a shout, leaned back in my chair, and sat there with a silly grin.

It hadn't been too long ago that board members looked forward to the day their term would be over. We had finally turned the corner. We'd come a long way from arguing over Communion cloths and retreads.

THREE

GUARDING THE GATE

It's too late to try to build unity after we've allowed a contentious or divisive person on the board. The damage has been done. I've found there is only one cure. We have to "guard the gate."

In the front of the room stood an old blackboard filled with names, each a potential nominee for the deacon board. There must have been twenty-five on the list, more than enough to fill the eight slots open. Then, just as the meeting was about to close, someone suggested a name. Dutifully, the chairman put it on the board.

Immediately, one of the other staff pastors leaned over to me and whispered, "They've got to be kidding!"

I nodded. All of us on the staff knew what his election would mean: Trouble!

He was a man of great personal charisma, an expert at "God talk." But behind the scenes he was contentious and critical. To make matters worse, he was a disciple and personal friend of one of the most rigid Bible teachers in the nation. Always quick to notice an interpretation or practice that differed from his favorite scholar's, he was apt to see a conspiracy behind any decision he didn't like.

We waited for the senior pastor, the chairman of the board, or someone to speak up, but no one did. Apparently, they figured it wasn't worth the risk of further alienating him and his friends. Besides that, his name was at the bottom of the list, too far down to have a serious chance of making the final ballot.

But one month later, there the man was, one of the final nominees presented at our annual congregational meeting. His name had worked its way up the list when many of those ahead of him had been unwilling or unable to run for office. Sure enough, he was elected to a three-year term, during which he became a major source of division. Fortunately, his term ended early when he left the church in a huff over a decision he didn't like.

Similar scenarios are played out every year in churches across the land. Each time, the unity of the board, and often of the entire church, suffers. While we usually direct our frustration at the person who causes the problem, the real culprit is actually quite different: a careless selection process.

Three Key Questions

I've found there is only one cure. We have to "guard the gate." It's too late to try to build unity after we've allowed a contentious or divisive person on the board. The damage has been done. At that point, the best we can hope for is damage control, not unity.

But, "guarding the gate" is delicate and dangerous. To pull it off effectively, some key questions need to be answered before we begin:

1. What is the board's primary purpose?
2. What are our minimum qualifications?
3. Who should guard the gate?

Representation or Leadership?

Is the primary purpose of a church board representation or leadership? Our answer has a significant impact on our potential for unity.

Many, if not most, churches, have opted for the representative model. It fits well with our American democratic principles, as well as one of our most cherished doctrines, the priesthood of believers. It insures that everyone has a chance to be heard, not just those who are powerful or well connected. And it is one way to guarantee the board stays in touch with the needs and desires of the congregation.

But a board of representatives also has its negatives. To begin with, the emphasis on representing the various interest groups in the body makes it difficult to justify keeping anyone off the board. From a representative perspective, any church member, no matter how divisive, has a right to be part of the leadership.

Second, it's harder to come to a consensus when faced with controversial issue. By definition, a representative board seeks to protect minority opinions; this often results in a stalemate rather than a solution.

Third, members of a representative board also can start to see themselves as lobbyists representing a specific constituency. Jack may become the champion of traditional worship, while John defends the youth. Meanwhile, Susan fights for the rights of the Sunday school. Forgotten in the fray can be the most important thing, finding and carrying out God's will.

For these reasons, and more, I've become a strong advocate of a leadership-oriented board. Compared to representative boards, leadership boards have a completely different agenda. Rather than figure out what everybody wants them to do, the members of a leadership board have only one focus: finding the best course of action and following it. They are more concerned with leading than responding to every whim of the congregation. When faced with a difficult decision, they ask first, not "How will people react?" but "What does God want us to do?"

This is not to say that a leadership board is unresponsive to the needs and concerns of the body. On the contrary, good leaders are always in touch with their people. But a good undershepherd never forgets he works for the Chief Shepherd, not the sheep.

Leadership boards have an easier time guarding the gate because they don't assume that every crusader who wants to radically change the direction of ministry has a right to lead. From their perspective, when it comes time to select board members, it doesn't matter whether a person represents a significant portion of the body.

What matters is whether that person can help the board fulfill its primary objective: knowing and implementing God's will.

Someone like the contentious nominee I described earlier would have no place in a leadership board. Despite his popularity, his record of taking every issue to the mat and castigating all who disagreed with him as heretics, would be enough reason to exclude him.

Leadership boards also have an easier time coming to a consensus when faced with a difficult issue. The reason? They have a common goal — discovering the will of the Lord — rather than conflicting individual goals of defending the rights of special interest groups.

When I came to North Coast, our board leaned heavily to the representative side of the scale. As a result, whenever we dealt with a controversial issue, the first thing most board members wanted to know was, "What will they think?" *They* represented a nebulous group of people who might complain if changes were made. No one knew who *they* were, and *they* seldom actually complained. But they were powerful; we spent a great deal of time every meeting seeking to keep them happy.

Now that we lean more heavily to the leadership side of the scale, instead of first asking what *they* would want us to do, we ask first what God would want us to do. Not only is this a better question; it's a tremendous unity builder. It undercuts any tendency to see ourselves as lobbyists, defending the rights of the young or the old, charismatics or non-charismatics, or any other group in the church.

I envision our board members as lobbyists for God. I often remind them that their job is to discern and carry out God's will, not the congregation's. Yet, ironically, the more we've moved in this direction, the greater our congregational unity and support have become.

For instance, when we changed our worship style, a number of folks objected. But since our leadership team was convinced that God wanted us to make the change and it was best for the church as a whole, we kept on moving. If we'd had a representative board, we'd probably still be debating the relative merits of contemporary and traditional music. As it was, once we made the decision, a few people who felt strongly left, but the vast majority went along with the change, particularly once they saw that our leadership team was united. It was enough to convince me that most people prefer to follow a loving and united group of leaders rather than bickering representatives — even when the decisions aren't always what they would choose.

What Are We Looking For?

Even if we're convinced that board members should serve as leaders rather than representatives, there is still another important question that needs to be answered before we can effectively guard the gate. What are our minimum qualifications going to be?

In many churches the primary qualification seems to be a willing heart. Anyone who faithfully supports the church and works hard eventually finds himself or herself rewarded with a seat on the board. While I know of no church that claims this as their method of selection, I know of plenty where it is, in fact, the way things are done.

Passages such as Acts 6, 1 Timothy 3, Titus 1, and 1 Peter 5 make it clear that a willing heart is not enough. There are spiritual qualifications, and they don't stop at being born again. They go way beyond to issues of character. While not everyone will agree on the exact interpretation and application of each passage, one thing is certain: the New Testament Church considered spiritual maturity to be a minimum qualification for leadership.

By spiritual maturity, I mean a life that consistently exhibits the character of Jesus Christ. That's not so much a matter of what a person knows as who he is. You'll notice that all of these passages deal more with character than giftedness, Bible knowledge, or zeal. We shouldn't be surprised, since some of the most self-centered and divisive people in the church are highly gifted, know the Bible inside out, and exhibit a zeal that puts most people to shame. And when they get on your board, watch out!

In attempting to apply these biblical standards to real situations, we need to strike a balance between two extremes. The first is to interpret these passages so no one can match up. I recall a pastor telling me that in his church of more than five hundred people, no one except he and another ordained minister were qualified to lead. It didn't dawn on him that this could be an indictment against his six years of ministry there.

The other danger is redefining or watering down the qualifications. I've found that in many churches, when someone fails to match up, many folks prefer to look the other way. Take, for instance, a board member whose family is falling apart. He'll receive sympathy and support, and maybe gossip, but he'll seldom be asked to step down. This despite passages that teach that a good home life is a necessary qualification for church leadership (1 Tim. 3:4–5, 12, and Titus 1:6). And how often have we seen board members who were contentious, self-willed, materialistic, or hotheaded, despite clear biblical warnings to not allow such people to lead?

What if there aren't enough qualified people willing or able to serve on the board? In that case, I recommend taking the best people available, and as the church grows and matures, slowly raising the standards.

As important as spiritual maturity is, to build a harmonious and effective leadership team there are other qualifications to look for as well. We've learned to ask two more questions:

1. Is this person in basic agreement with our current philosophy of ministry?

2. Will this person fit the leadership team we've already assembled?

If the answer to either is no, we've found it is a mistake to add the person to the board, no matter how spiritually mature he might be.

There is no guarantee that spiritually mature people will work well together. While they will usually share the same goals, there is no assurance they'll agree on the best way to get there. And when their convictions are strongly held and mutually exclusive (as were Paul and Barnabas' plans for dealing with John Mark), terrible things can happen. That's why it's important to have philosophical and relational qualifications as well as spiritual ones.

That doesn't mean every potential board member has to be in total agreement with everything we've previously decided or done. It does mean he has to be in agreement with the basic thrust of our ministry. Otherwise, conflict is inevitable.

As you can imagine, I met strong resistance when I first began to say this. Some folks couldn't understand why we would ever want to keep a spiritually mature person off the board simply because he disagreed with our current direction of ministry.

Frankly, I was amazed by their inconsistent thinking. Executives, who would have decried a mixture of divergent business philosophies on their company's board of directors, championed pluralism and a lack of homogeneity on the church's leadership board. Somehow they felt that church leaders could work well under conditions that would splinter any other group.

Imagine a pulpit committee deciding that the only qualifications necessary in a pastor were spiritual maturity and pastoral gifts. If they failed to consider the importance of a good fit as well, they'd be asking for trouble. It seldom works to bring a blue-collar pastor into a white-collar congregation. And a social activist (no matter how spiritual he may be) has little chance of succeeding in a church with a long history of bus ministries and prophecy conferences. Any wise pulpit committee, wanting to see a long and successful ministry, would obviously take these things into consideration. Is a good fit any less important when it comes to selecting lay leaders?

Determining a good fit can be time consuming, but it's vital. The more carefully our qualifications are thought out, and the more strictly they're held, the greater will be our chances of experiencing a harmonious and healthy board.

Who Should Guard the Gate?

There is one more question to answer before we're prepared to guard the gate: "Whom do we want to guard it?"

Make no mistake: the question is not, "Should someone guard the gate?" for someone already is. The questions are, "Are they doing a good job?" and "Are these the people we want to stand guard?"

Every church has gatekeepers. They are the folks who have the power to appoint or nominate; most often they are members of a nominating committee. Unfortunately, many churches underestimate their influence. Even churches that are very careful when it comes to choosing a governing board can be casual when it comes to deciding who will control the initial selection.

I was in one church when an announcement was made asking anyone who wanted to serve on the nominating committee to show up the next Tuesday night in the fellowship hall. If you came, you served. Other churches throw open the process to anyone willing to come to an all-church business meeting a month before the election. The method guarantees ineffective gate watching, because no matter how out of line a nomination may be, hardly anyone will be willing to speak out against it in a public meeting. I've also been in churches that figured the best selection committee was a cross section of the congregation — a housewife, career woman, businessman, senior citizen, and young person. The only qualification for service appeared to be matching the needed demographics.

Selecting leaders is too important to be treated casually. It demands the best people we've got. The nominating committee may be the most important committee in our church, because it serves like the headwaters of a river. If there's pollution upstream, it will eventually defile everything downstream. Frankly, if I could choose just one group in our church to be vested with the wisdom of Solomon, it wouldn't be our governing board, as much as they need God's wisdom. It would be our nominating committee.

One person, I believe, should always be involved in the process: the senior pastor. I realize that in some polities the pastor isn't allowed to take an official role in the nominating process, but even in those situations, a pastor can exercise a great deal of informal influence. By definition, a healthy and effective leadership team demands a good working relationship between the pastor and the board. It seems foolish to knowingly put someone on the board with whom the pastor is at personal or philosophical odds. Like saddling a coach with a general manager or assistant coaches who differ in philosophy, it's a ready-made recipe for failure.

I'm not suggesting the pastor hand-pick board members. But I am suggesting the pastor be given the opportunity to speak out against the nomination of someone who will cause nothing but conflict. Yet that opportunity will do us no good if we lack the courage to use it. The situation described at the beginning of this chapter would never have taken place if the senior pastor had spoken his mind. But he figured it wasn't his role to lead or dominate the committee, so he sat by quietly, hoping and praying that someone else would speak up and nix the nomination.

I've talked to many pastors who have served as an ex-officio member of the nominating committee but felt it was inappropriate to offer input. The way I look at it, if I'm not willing to speak up, why be there? And if I'm there and stay silent, I'm not sure I have a right to complain later about the people I have to work with. The nomination committee is like a wedding party: speak now or forever hold my peace.

One more thing I've discovered is that if the committee is going to be candid, I'll have to lead the way. No one wants to be accused of judging, and most folks are terrified that word of their veto might leak out. I remember the first time I vetoed a nomination. A godly man, with a totally different philosophy of leadership than the board's, had been put forward by numerous members of the congregation. When our nominating committee came to his name, there was an uncomfortable silence. He was a godly man who had faithfully served the church in the past, yet everyone knew he wouldn't fit the leadership team. The problems would be philosophical, not spiritual, but problems nonetheless. After what seemed like an eternity, I swallowed hard and spoke up, "I don't think we should have him run; we'll end up spending all our meetings going around in circles."

Once that was on the table, a couple of others were quick to agree. After a brief discussion we came to a unanimous consensus to nominate someone else. It was obvious that others felt as strongly as I did, but no one had said a word until I broke the ice. Our consensus, a wise one, would have remained unspoken and unacted upon.

Since then, others have begun to speak out. No longer am I the only one, or even the first, because a standard of candor has been set.

Obviously, my decision to get involved in the process holds some risk. As one friend keeps asking, "How can you do that without being killed?" Actually, it's never created a problem. The reason? We keep strict confidentiality. Since our nominating committee is made up of top-quality people, the members don't have a problem remembering, "What is said here should remain here." And in case they forget, I remind them before every meeting!

But I'll admit that choosing to get involved in the selection process can be risky for a pastor. Secrets are hard to keep, and a pastoral veto has the potential for creating hurt. So I'm always very careful with what I say and how I say it. I hope things I say won't be repeated, but I make sure I can live with them if they are.

My decision to become an outspoken member of the nominating committee didn't come easily. It went against the advice of some of my most trusted mentors. But, after prayerful and careful consideration, I figured I had little to lose. I'd witnessed the results of silence too many times.

How One Church Does It

Many of you are probably wondering how these principles work in real life. For that reason, I'll briefly describe our selection process. Your polity and circumstances will dictate which parts of this process fit. The process is offered not as a prescription, but as a description of how one church has taken seriously the need for guarding the gate.

In our case, our elder board serves as the final nominating committee. While there are obviously some potential problems with a standing board functioning as its own nominating committee, these are the best people we've got, so we use them.

Each week during the month preceding our nominations, the bulletin contains a nomination form. We ask all regular attenders to fill out one and drop it in the offering plate or mail it into the office. Our newsletter and pulpit announcements reinforce the importance of picking people who are qualified spiritually and philosophically.

At the end of the month, our elder board goes over the congregational nominations, as well as those from each pastor and elder. We go through the combined list and eliminate anyone who obviously doesn't fit: in our case, nonmembers, people who have been in the church less than a year, and any person with a glaring spiritual or emotional problem. We then go over the remaining names asking everyone to give a candid response. Character flaws aren't always obvious; often, only one or two of us will be aware of a shaky marriage, a hot temper, or a lack of discretion. We also ask ourselves how well these people fit our philosophy of ministry and leadership team. (Frankly, few people fail this test. Most of those who would have long since left the church.)

A second part of the process is deciding how many openings we have, which depends on how many current board members plan to continue and whether we need to increase the size of the board. One advantage we have is that our constitution calls only for a minimum of five elders. While that's too few in our situation, it gives us freedom to increase or decrease the size of the board based on our needs, rather than an arbitrary number of slots.

Next, we list our choices in order of priority. We ask the first person on the list if he'd be willing to serve. If not, we go down the list to the next person, and on to the end of the list of qualified nominees. If all those on the list said no, something that has never happened, we wouldn't add anyone that year. Under no circumstances would we knowingly add someone who was unqualified simply because we had an opening to fill.

Finally, we present our nominees to the congregation at our annual meeting. Each nominee is voted on — yes or no — individually. So far, we've chosen not to have two people run for the same position. I find the main reason churches run two people against each other is to give the congregation a choice. They don't want people to feel that their leaders are being forced on them. But as long as we give people the opportunity to vote yes or no on each candidate, they don't seem to mind.

In fact, a commitment to always run more than one person for each position can undo a careful selection process. Most churches don't have enough top-notch people to run two candidates for every opening. As a result, nominating committees put unqualified people on the ballot and pray the congregation won't elect them. We prefer to put forward our top choices without apology and let the congregation confirm or reject them.

Running two candidates for every office also tends to keep some excellent people off the board. Only those who serve in highly visible positions or who have good name recognition end up being elected, particularly in larger churches in which there is no way for the members to know everyone. Despite all I've said, however, I'm not against running two people for an office if there are enough qualified people so that it doesn't matter who wins. But in the real world, that is seldom the case.

Anyway, that's the process we use. It works for us. While we are committed to the principles, we have no great commitment to the methodology. We'll change or adapt it anytime we find a better way to insure quality control in our selection process.

The bottom line is to do whatever is necessary to get our best people on the board. Winning teams need winning players. Even Knute Rockne couldn't win with the wrong material. Neither can our church board.

FOUR

DEVELOPING THREE KEY TRAITS IN YOUR BOARD

I've noticed that almost every dysfunctional board conspicuously lacks three traits. In contrast, these same three traits dominate the decision-making process when a board is healthy and effective. So I've made developing these three traits a top priority.

Every year, the nominating committee asks my friend Bob to run for a term on the church council. Every year he says, "No, not this year."

Bob would make an ideal board member: he's a mature Christian and natural leader, and he's committed to the church, generously supporting it with both time and money. But Bob remembers the one time he said yes. "The late-night meetings and arguments were more than I could handle," he says. "On the way home I'd be frustrated and angry, and the next morning I'd be exhausted at work. Worse, I found myself growing cynical. It took me a couple of years to recover my spiritual equilibrium."

The board at Bob's church was dysfunctional. The symptoms are easily recognized: frequent tardiness, absenteeism, and a perennial problem securing enough qualified people willing to serve. The predictable result is a chronic leadership crisis — a shortage caused not so much by a scarcity of good leaders as by a scaring of the good ones away.

Over the years, I've served on, worked with, or been around many dysfunctional boards. I've noticed that in almost every instance there has been a conspicuous lack of three traits. In contrast, these same three traits dominate the decision-making process when a board is healthy and effective. So I've made their development a top priority.

Teamwork

As any sports fan knows, the best players don't always win the championship. The best team does. What's true on the field is also true in the board room. When everyone knows, accepts, and fulfills his role on the leadership team, the odds for success escalate.

I've found there are two common saboteurs of teamwork: lack of a clearly defined leader, and failure to distinguish between designing and evaluating a ministry.

One thing every team needs is a clearly defined leader. Teamwork depends on it. Someone has to keep everyone headed in the same direction.

I compare the leader to a point guard on a basketball team. Directing the offense falls on his shoulders. That doesn't mean the off guard, forwards, or center can't initiate a play or fast break, but most of the time they'll look to him to take the lead. In a church, a leader sets the agenda, general tone, and direction for ministry. When a tough problem or exciting opportunity comes along, everyone knows to whom to look for direction.

This type of leader is very different from an authoritarian leader. An authoritarian leader expects to be obeyed; an initiating leader expects to be heard. Once he's made his point, he leaves it up to the team whether to accept, modify, or reject his advice. He's what my friend Charles Bradshaw calls a "powerful servant." In other words, he's a leader, not a monarch.

As we'll see in the next chapter, the senior pastor is usually the person best suited for this position. But obviously, there are times when a church's polity, history, or other factors make that impossible or not advisable. What's important is that one person lead. Dysfunctional boards tend to have two or three people vying for the leader position, resulting in attacks on one another rather than the problems at hand.

I realize some people advocate a leaderless board as the ultimate expression of unity and teamwork. I once counted myself among them. But I think I erred on two counts.

First, I failed to acknowledge the role of de facto leaders. What I called a leaderless board was often far from leaderless. For instance, I know of one church that prided itself on not having an officially designated leader. But title or no, it was obvious who the real leader was — so much so that most people said, "I go to Gene Johnson's church." As long as Gene was around, the "leaderless" board worked marvelously. His charisma, knowledge, and arbitration skills kept everyone headed in the same direction. But once Gene left, so did the board's teamwork. Within two years they were embroiled in controversy.

Second, I underestimated the fury of a storm. When a crisis hits a church, people need to know who's in charge. As long as there's smooth sailing, there is no great need for a captain; anyone can man the helm. But once a storm hits, someone has to take charge, and when he does, it's important the crew has no qualms about his ability or right to lead.

Settling on a clearly defined and accepted leader is one of the first steps to greater teamwork.

Something else that can sabotage teamwork is the failure to distinguish between designing and evaluating.

Designing is a solo task; it needs to be carried out by one person (or at the most two or three people). Evaluating, on the other hand, is a group task; the more, the merrier.

When an entire board tries to design, create, or generate new programs, it's headed for failure and frustration. There are good reasons why people joke about planning by committee. It's no accident that the world's greatest inventions, musical compositions, and artistic masterpieces have come from inspired individuals, not blue-ribbon committees.

At Bob's church, whenever a crisis or golden opportunity loomed, his pastor came to the board and said, "What do you think we ought to do?" That put the board in an impossible position. With thirteen members, they were too large and diverse a group to develop an effective proposal. Most of the time, after pooling ideas, they'd argue late into the night over how to combine them into a workable plan. Eventually they'd table the discussion until the next meeting.

Teamwork doesn't mean everybody does everything; it means everyone does what he does best. Translated to a board setting, it means letting the leader, staff, or a small group propose strategy. Then the entire group can evaluate, fine-tune, and modify the plans — things larger groups do well.

We've learned to strenuously avoid designing by committee. In fact, we have no standing committees outside of our elder board. When we have a problem or opportunity, we turn it over to an individual or *small* group: a pastor, a staff member, a fellow elder, or a task force. We leave it to them to propose an innovative solution.

Once the designers have a proposal, the board moves into action. We evaluate. If anything is wrong or missing, we can usually find it. Sometimes we even scrap the idea and move in a whole new direction. But the key to the board's effectiveness is having something to react to rather than trying to work from a blank slate.

For a church board to fully experience teamwork, I believe it needs to accept that initiating and designing ministry are individual skills, while evaluating and critiquing are group skills. Then it can allow individuals to do what they do best, and concentrate on the group activities it does best. The result? Shorter meetings, less frustration, and a more innovative ministry.

Courage

A second mark of a healthy board is courage. When a tough decision has to be made, people aren't afraid to make it. They realize that's what they've been called to do. In contrast, dysfunctional boards often are dominated by fear. They find it safer to say no and to maintain the status quo.

Why do some boards lack courage? One, groups tend to be more conservative than individuals, more cautious and oriented toward the past. Two, most board members take their responsibilities as a sacred trust. They are hesitant to take unnecessary chances, alienate members, or make a mistake. These are commendable concerns, but when taken to an extreme, they can paralyze the decision-making process.

I've found that whenever a board lacks the courage to lead, it tends to lean too heavily upon two opinion-gathering devices: (1) surveys and (2) congregational meetings.

Surveys seldom give us the accurate information we think we're getting. Not long after I arrived at the church, I used a survey to gauge interest in small-group Bible studies. I was thrilled to discover over half the congregation wanted to be in one. I gathered leaders, and we put together a series of studies. However, when it came time to sign up, hardly anyone did. Only later did I realize what had happened. People had answered my survey with what they perceived to be the "right answer." They felt they ought to be in a Bible study, so they hesitated to check the box saying, "No, I won't be able to participate."

Another problem with surveys is that by nature they zero in on what people want, not what they need. Ask a group what to study next and invariably you'll find prophecy and a host of controversial subjects at the top of their list. Teaching on prophecy is hardly most people's greatest need. A pastor who planned his preaching schedule around such surveys would be derelict in his duties as a spiritual leader. The same goes for a board that relied too heavily upon opinion polls when making decisions or designing a ministry.

Another tool that can be misused is congregational meetings. I'm not talking about an annual meeting or a constitution that puts ultimate authority in the hands of the congregation. That's the system my church uses, and I'm not only comfortable with it, I also advocate it. My concern is with situations where the leaders turn all but the most insignificant decisions back to the congregation. I realize that questioning the effectiveness of congregational meetings is, to some, tantamount to heresy. But I wonder if asking an entire congregation to be intricately involved in the decision-making process is the best way to do things. It's a sure way to increase the likelihood of conflict and division.

In all but the smallest churches, it's unreasonable to expect everyone to come to the meetings. As a rule of thumb, the larger the congregation, the smaller the percentage of people who show up. As a result, it's easy for a small faction of chronic complainers and malcontents to wield an inordinate amount of power.

That's what happened at Ron's church. In the early years, the small flock met once a month to hammer out issues and okay expenditures. It worked so well they wrote it into the constitution. Forty years later they still held a congregational business meeting on the first Wednesday of every month. Hardly anyone showed, but those who did haggled over every nickel and dime, in essence holding a church of four hundred hostage. Why didn't the rest of the congregation show up and put an end to it? They (1) lacked the time, (2) hated meetings, (3) abhorred conflict, and (4) trusted their elected leaders. So they tried to ignore the undercurrent of hostility, hoping it would go away.

Those who champion lots of churchwide business meetings assume that the more people involved in the decision-making process, the better the final decision will be. But there is no way an entire congregation can work through a complex issue as carefully as a small board. The result will almost always be more heat than light.

That's why our board never asks the congregation to debate a number of options. Instead, we bring a single proposal and ask the people to approve or reject it. This is true whether it's our annual budget, a proposed addition to our staff, or any other item.

We believe it's our job as leaders to dig through the facts, compare the consequences of various options, and come up with a plan. Then it's the congregation's prerogative to accept or reject that plan. That's not to say we don't give the congregation an opportunity to offer input or ask tough questions. But it's our goal to get any debate, concerns, or proposed changes on the table long before the congregation gathers to vote.

We accomplish this in a couple of ways. First, we inundate people with Sunday announcements and congregational letters to make sure they know exactly what we are proposing and why. Second, we hold question-and-answer sessions a few weeks before the meeting, so everyone can make suggestions, register complaints, or clarify issues. Frankly, not many people show up at these informational meetings. But the meetings give people a place to vent feelings, and they give us an opportunity to interact with critics away from the emotionally charged setting of a congregational meeting.

The result? Boring congregational meetings. Most last ten to fifteen minutes. I can't remember the last time someone raised his voice or got mad. We've found that most church members want the board to lead. They have no desire to get mired in the sticky details; and they don't like the confusion, conflict, and inefficiency of large-group decision making. As long as they have opportunity for input, and the authority to say yea or nay on major decisions, they're happy.

Healthy boards realize this and lead. If we're going to develop courage in our board, we need to help the board not to shift its leadership back to the congregation.

Trust

The final key trait I want our board to display is trust. Every board I've worked with has had a basic bent toward either trust or suspicion. Dysfunctional boards ask "Why?" Healthy boards ask "Why not?"

What caused the difference? In most cases, it was a choice. Dysfunctional boards chose the role of watchdog, making sure no one got by with anything. Predictably, they had an abundance of adversarial relationships. On the other hand, healthy boards chose trust.

How can we develop trust in our board?

To begin with, by helping the board avoid micromanagement. A consuming attention to detail reveals only one thing: lack of trust in the competence and judgment of others. A board develops trust as it keeps its focus on the big picture — setting direction, making policy. Trusting boards don't argue over what kind of tires to put on the church van. They leave that decision to the people who maintain and drive the van.

One friend served on a board that insisted upon approving every expenditure over ten dollars. They spent so much time on the budget they never had time for the more important issues — prayer, strategy, and vision.

Overattention to the details of ministry creates a bottleneck. Nothing gets done until the board has a chance to meet. For those on the front lines that can be incredibly frustrating, particularly when they need to make a decision or purchase now. It creates a perception that the board is an obstacle to progress, something to get around, an enemy rather than an ally.

Micromanagement also tends to undercut creativity. By definition, a creative idea goes against the grain. It's different from the way we've done things. But by the time micromanagers have finished with an idea, it's usually rather conventional. For example, the pastor of a neighboring church wanted to know why home fellowships had worked well for us so that he could start some. I was careful to point out that much of the success was due to some creative twists we'd given the program. Later, I found out that his board had liked the idea, but unfortunately, they were micromanagers. By the time they were finished reworking the idea, not one of the unconventional aspects was left. The result was a plain vanilla program that never excited anyone.

Sometimes in the early days of a ministry, micromanagement is a necessity. But as a church grows, the board needs to move away from managing details to overseeing the big picture. The transition depends on their willingness to trust others.

Healthy boards give people freedom to do things in whatever way they deem best. In matters of taste, style, or methodology, they don't butt in. They let those who have the responsibility for a ministry also have the authority to carry it out.

The Hessian mercenaries understood this principle as well as anyone. The three guiding principles in their Rules of Combat would serve any board well.

1. The mission's objective and any constraints must be made explicit by the commander [the board] *in advance.* In other words, everyone has to know the rules ahead of time — both the goal and the limits of their freedom. For instance, our youth associates need to know how we're going to judge the success of their program. Will it be by attendance, number of new Christians, signs of spiritual growth, or the percentage of church kids that buy in? And what are their constraints? Do they have a budget? How much? Are there any programs or ministries they must provide (Sunday school, camps, or a set number of socials)?

We use a tool called a "position focus" to spell this out.[1] But any good job description will do. What's important is that both staff and key volunteers know explicitly what the board expects them to accomplish.

2. Individuals are to be given the freedom to pursue the objective as they think best in the light of local conditions. No one knows better than those on the front line what will and won't work. Most of us have had the experience of being forced to do something in a way that we knew was less than best. I remember once being forced to use a certain speaker, who I knew would be boring, at a conference I was planning. Worse, I had to emcee the meetings and introduce the speaker. That put me in a compromising position. If I promoted the conference, knowing full well our people would get little or nothing out of it, my credibility would suffer. If I downplayed the conference, and no one came, I'd have a financial disaster on my hands. Needless to say, the board's interference was not appreciated.

This principle is particularly important when dealing with staff. Why hire an expert if we aren't going to let him do his thing? When our board hires someone, we look for the wisest and most gifted person we can find. For us to kibitz and control the details of the ministry would waste his or her gifts and indict our judgment in hiring.

3. The freedom of officers [ministry leaders] *is to be limited only when it's essential in order to coordinate their actions.* Keeping everyone moving in the same direction is one of the board's primary jobs. Sometimes that calls for reining in a particular ministry. I know of one church where the music program became so large that the splashy programs and travel tours left few volunteers for anything else. So when the director asked for permission to raise funds for another bus and still more sound equipment the board had to say no.

Occasionally, a special emphasis or program will also mandate that freedom be temporarily set aside. During a missions emphasis we can't have the youth group off on a ski trip, or the women's ministry hosting a weekend retreat. But other than times like these, it's hands off. Even if we doubt an idea will work, we try to give people the freedom to give it a shot. That's what trust is all about.

---

[1] Available From MasterPlanningGroup.com

FIVE

CLARIFYING THE PASTOR'S ROLE

Am I supposed to be the leader, taking charge, setting the agenda for ministry? Am I supposed to be the church's employee, waiting for orders? Or am I the chaplain, carrying out the spiritual duties assigned by the board and not getting involved in the decision-making process?

Navigating my way through unfamiliar streets, my thoughts darted between the task at hand — finding a pancake house at the edge of town — and the opportunities ahead of me as the new pastor of a small, Southern California church.

After eight years as a youth pastor and assistant pastor, I was excited by the challenge. As I pulled my Toyota into the restaurant's parking lot, I was full of ideas, energy, and enthusiasm. The chairman of our board had been in Europe while I candidated and was called, but at this pancake house we finally would have the chance to get acquainted.

After initial pleasantries, the chairman asked me what I had in mind for the church. For thirty minutes, I shared my dreams and vision.

When I finished, he leaned across the table. "Son," he said, "don't get too many fancy ideas. You just preach and pray. We'll run the church. And don't dig your roots too deep, either, because it's a good idea to move on every three or four years."

I was stunned. Based on the interviewing process, I'd assumed people were looking to me to set the direction for our ministry. But it was painfully obvious that as far as he was concerned, I was an employee, not a leader. And something told me his opinions weren't to be taken lightly. Maybe it was the three offices he held — board chairman, treasurer, and finance elder.

What's My Role?

Driving home, I knew we had a serious problem. Each of us saw himself as occupying the same role, the initiating leader.

Many, if not most, leadership teams experience such role confusion at one time or another, particularly when there's a new group of lay leaders or a new pastor has been brought onto the scene.

I asked myself questions: *Am I supposed to be the leader, taking charge, setting the agenda for ministry? Am I supposed to be the church's employee, waiting for orders? Or am I the chaplain, carrying out the spiritual duties assigned by the board and not getting involved in the decision-making process?* All my instincts told me that for the sake of an effective and growing ministry, I needed to function as an initiating leader. But before this could happen, the board and I needed to answer three key questions.

Whose Church Is It?

When a pastor finds, as I did, that some of the lay leaders don't want him to lead, it usually indicates that they see him as an outsider, a hired hand to take care of spiritual chores. And no one who cares a lick about his church is going to hand it over to an outsider.

Obviously, a church doesn't belong to anyone. It's the Lord's alone. But there is a legitimate sense in which people speak of a church as "their church." Those who have poured significant time, money, and energy into a local congregation rightfully feel a sense of ownership. After all, they have demonstrated love and concern for it.

A new pastor usually has an easy time leading these people — as long as he leads them along the same road. But let him (or her) suggest a change in direction, and he'll quickly learn how little real leadership he's been granted. It doesn't matter if the changes are significant or minor; people soon will start asking, "What's he trying to do to *our* church?"

How important that pronoun is! Until the leaders are convinced it is as much my church as theirs, they will not let me function as their leader. A respected, influential, and honored outsider, perhaps, but an outsider nonetheless.

To overcome this, pastors need two things: time and a personal commitment to that local body.

There isn't much we can do about the passage of time. And exactly how much time is needed depends on factors such as the age of the church, the length of the previous pastorate, and our age in relation to the other leaders' ages.

But demonstrating commitment to the church is totally up to us. Until the board members are convinced the pastor is as committed to the church as they are, they won't let him lead.

Perceptions are sometimes more important than the reality. When we came to the church, my wife and I were committed to the church and community for the long haul, for better or for worse. We often said so during the candidating process. Yet, even after I had been around long enough to expect trust and tenure, I found some board members still resisting my leadership role.

Why? Because no matter what I said, their past experiences led them to believe I wouldn't stick around. Our board chairman, for example, had seen many a pastor come and go during his years of committee and board work. And since our church was small and struggling, and I was young and "on my way up," it's no wonder he was hesitant to turn over the reins. I would have been, too.

The board members had to see me demonstrate my commitment with my finances, my use of time, and my decisions to stay with the church even when opportunities to move came along.

Lay leaders may give lots of other reasons for resisting a pastor's leadership, but the real issue is usually a concern that he isn't as committed to the long-term ministry of the church as they are.

Frankly, they are often right. When a tough crisis comes along, many pastors bail out. One denominational study found a pastoral crisis occurred every year and a half. Not coincidentally, pastors from this same group moved on an average of every eighteen to twenty months. We may speak of a calling, but if our résumés reveal something that looks strangely like a career track, our lay leaders will know it.

Obviously, many pastors can't stay for the long haul, due to personal, geographical, and even denominational constraints. That's okay, as long as we don't usurp the authority and leadership of those who will be there for the long run. If, for whatever reason, we know our stay will be short, we need to let someone else take on the role of primary, initiating leader. A more appropriate role for us might be that of an influential consultant.

Aaron, for example, serves in a denomination that moves him to a new parish every three to five years. He sees no reason to battle for the reins; he knows he would lose. So when he arrives at a new church, he quickly tries to find out who the real power brokers are. Then he pours his life into theirs. He knows that long after he's gone, they'll still be running the show, so he tries to influence rather than lead.

Pastors who want to take the responsibility of strong leadership have to give up the privilege of loose commitment. Only adequate time and our demonstrated commitment will help boards see that the church is not only theirs, but also ours.

Who's Best Qualified to Lead?

Even if the pastor is as committed to the church as the rest of the board is, most lay leaders will want to know why the pastor should be the leader. Why not the chairman of the board, another lay person, or the entire board working together?

The answer is easy. In most cases, the pastor is best qualified to lead, not necessarily by virtue of age, intelligence, spirituality, or force of personality, for many board members can surpass their pastor in these areas, but by virtue of two key factors: time and training.

As a full-time pastor, I'm immersed in the day-to-day ministry of the church. Unlike any of my board members, I'm thinking about our problems and opportunities full-time. I have the time to plan, pray, consult, and solve problems.

To lead, a person needs to know the organization inside out — how the parts fit together and how each will be affected by proposed changes. And that takes time, lots of it. In all but the smallest churches, it can't be done on a spare-time basis. In a church with a multiple staff, Lyle Schaller claims, it takes between fifty and sixty hours a week.[1]

Not that our board members are incapable of leading an organization. That's what a number do for a living. But they do it on a full-time basis. None would think of trying to do it in his or her spare time. Yet that is exactly what happens in a church where the board or a powerful lay leader tries to take on the primary leadership role.

I also have a decided advantage when it comes to training. Like most pastors, my formal education and ongoing studies have equipped me specifically to lead a church. Add to that a network of fellow pastors and church leaders, and I have a wealth of information from which to draw. When a church faces a tough situation or golden opportunity, the pastor is the one most likely to have been exposed to a similar situation. If not, he'll usually know where to find out what the experts recommend.

By contrast, most board members are limited in their exposure to other ministries. They don't have the time to read the literature. And their network of experts is usually limited to a previous pastor or two. Because the church is spiritually centered, volunteer run, and educationally focused, it's different from any other organization, and as a rule, the pastor has more training in how to lead it than anyone else.

Are there exceptions? Certainly, but that's the point: they're *exceptions.* A friend tried to model his church after one with an incredibly strong and competent group of lay leaders. In his model church, the pastor simply prayed, taught, and counseled, while the elders took care of everything else. There was no need for strong pastoral leadership, he told me, if you picked the right people and discipled them properly. But he failed to notice that the key elders in his model church were self-employed and independently wealthy. They had all the time in the world, and they attended seminars and seminary classes and read in their spare time.

His elders, on the other hand, all had jobs that called for fifty to sixty hours a week. They had neither the time nor the training to take a strong leadership role. As long as my friend waited for the elders to take charge, the church floundered.

What about pastors who feel they aren't cut out to take a strong leadership role?

In a smaller church, a key lay person might be able to fill the role. While it's not the ideal (due to the time and training constraints we've just looked at, as well as the problems it might create for the next pastor, should he want to take back the reins), it sometimes has to be done if the church is going to move ahead.

A staff member might be another option. I know one church where the associate pastor was a stronger leader than the senior pastor, so the pastor let him lead. They had known each other for a long time, and they had a great deal of mutual trust and respect, so it worked well for them.

One thing won't work: The pastor can't be a Dr. Jekyll/Mr. Hyde leader, someone who abdicates leadership and later jumps in to take over. That only confuses, embarrasses, and annoys the people who have been pushed aside in the attempt to rescue the situation.

In short, the role of primary leader needs to be filled on a protracted basis, and usually the pastor is the best person to fill it.

Can a Strong Leader Be Controlled?

Before being allowed to take a strong leadership role, most pastors have to clear one more hurdle: the fear of domination. It doesn't matter how committed or qualified a pastor might be, his or her leadership will be resisted if people think it smacks of domination.

Most people fear a dictatorship, even a benevolent one. Nearly everyone has a horror story of a strong leader gone bad. And the fear is even greater in churches, like mine, that have a heritage of congregational government. To some folks, strong leadership and domination are synonymous. Before they'll let a pastor lead, they have to be thoroughly convinced that appropriate checks and balances are firmly in place.

As far as I'm concerned, those fears are justified. I know my sin nature too well to want *carte blanche*. I've committed myself to follow three key guidelines — not only to keep me in line, but also to allay the fears of those who are most suspicious of a strong leader.

1. I present first drafts, not final proposals. I don't mean that I offer half-baked ideas or suggestions off the top of my head. My first drafts are carefully thought out and forcefully presented. But I don't confuse them with God's final revealed will on a subject. That's something the board and I will determine together.

It's easy for a strong leader to make it sound as if every idea he has came directly from God, completely developed, needing nothing but the board's approval. But that puts the board in an awkward position — not fellow leaders seeking to know God's will, but judges passing judgment on God's ideas. When that happens, boards that hate conflict become a rubber stamp. Those that fear domination dig in and become an adversary.

When Don sought to lead his board, for example, he presented his ideas as straight from the Lord. Fearing domination, some of the board members began to resist his leadership. Even when they might otherwise have agreed with his proposals, they put up a fight. It was the only way they knew to keep him from taking total control.

In Don's eyes, the board was carnal. After a few years, he left to go to a church where people were more open to God's leading. But he soon found the same thing happening again.

Sadly, the resistance wasn't so much to Don's ideas as to his style. If he had offered the same ideas as first-draft proposals, many of them would have been supported.

2. *I keep no secrets from the board.* When I keep something from the board, perhaps because of its sensitive nature, I'm putting them at a decided disadvantage. If they make a different decision than they would have with all the facts, they've been duped and manipulated.

For instance, I used to see no reason why the board needed to know the details of the spiritual and moral struggles our people went through. That was privileged communication between pastor and parishioner. But when it came to making decisions about people, the board and I had two sets of information.

I now ask most people who come to me for help if I can share the situation with the elders if I need to. I'm not the least bit apologetic. If it's a significant issue, I simply say, "The elders need to know about this. Can I tell them?" Almost everyone says yes. If not, I honor their request, but I also suggest they go to someone else for counsel because the elders and I jointly shepherd the flock, and we can't do our job if we keep secrets from one another.

To my surprise, no has one has ever gotten upset or angry or left the church over this. In fact, most folks seem to appreciate it.

That doesn't mean I share every gory detail or all the little problems that arise, but I have permission to share information the board needs to know in order to make wise decisions.

I learned the importance of this guideline the hard way. During my third year at the church, I found myself accused of misleading and manipulating the board. Though my motives were pure, I stood guilty as charged.

We had hired a staff member who wasn't working out. During his first year, I received numerous complaints about his failure to follow through on plans and commitments. I kept the comments to myself, figuring it was my role to be a staff advocate. But before long, the board heard some complaints on their own. At a later budget meeting, a couple of elders suggested we let this staff member go. During the discussion, I made no mention of the calls I'd received or my own growing frustration. Instead, I pointed out the good things he had done (and there were many). We ended up giving him a raise!

But a year later, I realized things weren't going to work out. Along with the other problems, now the staff member and I weren't getting along. So I went to the board and told them I thought we should make a change. They were perplexed. How could I defend his work one year and ask for his release the next? When I explained what really had been going on, some board members became indignant. Why hadn't they been informed before?

The truth was, I didn't trust them to deal with the information. I was afraid they might overreact. But that only revealed the hollowness of my claims to believe in a leadership team. I had taken on the role not of a strong leader but a manipulator. I promised myself it would never happen again.

3. I follow the board's advice. Some people confuse leadership with infallibility. They assume that submitting to others means abdicating their leadership role.

Jim is a case in point. Whenever his board resisted an idea or asked him to go in another direction, he found a way to get around their advice. It never occurred to him that God might want him to follow the board's direction. It's no surprise that Jim constantly complained about his board's unwillingness to follow his lead. What he called *leadership* they called a refusal to cooperate. They never did develop a relationship of trust.

I've committed myself to follow the board's advice not only because I want to avoid the resistance that comes with a domineering leadership style, but also because I want to be a wise leader. Both life and Scripture have taught me that wisdom is found in heeding counsel, even when I think it's wrong.

Even when I'm right on an issue, I can be wrong on the timing. Often, the Lord has used the board's hesitancy to slow me down. For instance, the board's caution caused me to move much more slowly with changing our worship music from traditional to contemporary. The switch was accomplished without even a minor church fight because it was done at the right time and at the right pace. Submitting to their will, rather than looking for a way to get around it, has kept many a great idea from premature birth.

There are only two circumstances under which I wouldn't submit to the board's direction. First, if they wanted me to violate what I understood to be the clear teaching of Scripture, as happened to one pastor whose board wanted to financially support an organization that was pro-abortion. Second, if they asked me to disobey what I understood to be the clear and unmistakable voice of the Lord. In the last nine years that's happened only once.

I was pushing for us to hire someone from within the body to fill an associate pastor position. While he was a gifted and anointed man of God, at that time he lacked a seminary education and had never worked in a church. Understandably, some of the board members were hesitant; they wanted to hire someone who had been around the block before.

But one night, driving home from a meeting, I felt God made it absolutely clear to me that we were supposed to hire Mike. It was one of those supernatural moments when you know beyond a shadow of a doubt that God has spoken. So I went to the board and told them, "I strongly feel that God wants us to hire Mike."

Some of them were taken aback, but they didn't argue. "Fine," they said, "we'll present him to the congregation."

It turned out to be one of the most important decisions we've made. Within months, even those who had voiced the most concern over his qualifications were singing his praises. Yet I'm sure the board never would have gone along with me if I hadn't followed their direction previously, even when it differed from mine.

I've found the more successful and experienced we become as leaders, the easier it is to ignore those who disagree. But anyone who's tempted not to follow the board's advice should consider the options. If he is lucky, the board members will dig in their heels, providing a check against tyranny. If he's not, they'll let him have everything he wants, a fate much worse than staunch resistance. Sooner or later, he'll make a terrible decision, and there will be no one to stop him.

Research has shown that strong pastoral leadership is a key ingredient in a healthy and growing church. But it can't be demanded or taken. It has to be granted. The board needs to be convinced that (1) we're committed to the church, (2) we are qualified to lead, and (3) we desire to lead, not dominate.

Asking these three questions, and thoughtfully answering them, will help lead us to more effective pastor-board relationships.

SIX

EQUIPPING THE SAINTS TO LEAD

Training the board is one of the most effective ways to increase unity and efficiency. Unfortunately, most board members receive, at best, a cursory introduction to their task.

When Tim entered the ministry, he honestly looked forward to working with board members. Even though he'd heard his share of war stories, he figured his case would be different. As long as good people were elected and carefully discipled, he saw no reason why he and the board couldn't get along famously.

But five years later, as I talked with him, Tim wasn't so sure. Instead of partners, the board members seemed like adversaries. It no longer surprised him when even his best ideas were rejected outright. Sometimes he wondered if his board members understood ministry at all.

Odds are, they didn't.

Not that they weren't sharp people or good leaders. They were. But no one had trained them for their role. They had never been exposed to the unique principles and requirements of leading a spiritual and volunteer organization like the church. That was left for Tim and his fellow professionals to learn at Bible school and seminary. Everyone else was expected to figure it out on their own.

Tim's training, and their lack of it, caused them to view issues from radically different perspectives. They were suffering from what I call "educational separation." And with every new book Tim read and every seminar he attended, he slowly widened the gap between the way he saw the church and the way his lay leaders did.

When Tim told me about his predicament, I understood. Early in my ministry, I had faced a similar situation. It seemed the more I learned about ministry, the more I found myself frustrated with board members who had never been exposed to the material, much less bought into it.

Overcoming Educational Separation

Searching for some way to close the gap, I decided to set up an on-the-job training program to expose our board members to the same insights and principles I had been exposed to during my own training for ministry. But instead of focusing on the standard biblical and doctrinal themes, I zeroed in on practical theology, the stuff I studied in my pastoral ministry and Christian education classes.

Almost immediately, the gap in our perceptions of ministry began to close. Now that they were being trained like pastors, many of our board members started to think like pastors. Even when we disagreed, we had an easier time understanding and appreciating each other's viewpoint. Most important, we made better informed and wiser decisions.

Over the years, we've tackled a variety of subjects, church growth, educational theory, group dynamics, management styles, and the role of New Testament elders, to name a few. We've read articles and books by Lyle Schaller, Rick Warren, and others; and we've reviewed books like *Why Men Hate Going to Church* and secular books such as Jim Collin's *Good to Great*. Also, whenever I attend a particularly impactful seminar or conference, I summarize for the board any significant insights.

Training the board makes a difference, a big one. It's one of the most effective ways to increase unity and efficiency. Unfortunately, most board members receive, at best, a cursory introduction to their task.

In this chapter I want to look at the big picture: why training is so important, and what principles guide the way I train. In the next chapter, I'll explain the details of how our training program actually works.

A Biblical and Practical Priority

From my perspective, training board members should be a top priority for both biblical and practical reasons. First, the Bible mandates it. Ephesians 4:11–13 is a case in point. This popular text can be found on bulletin covers, letterheads, and logos. It articulates the Christian leader's responsibility to equip the rest of the body to do the work of the ministry. Increasingly, in the church, the one-man show is out, something I find refreshing and biblical.

But I also find that in our rush to equip lay people to study the Word, evangelize, teach, and counsel, we often have neglected to train them for one of the most vital areas of ministry: leadership. As important as the usual training is, training for leadership is more so. I agree with Bobb Biehl: "Every organization is a direct reflection of its leadership, for better or worse."[1]

It's no accident that Jesus spent the bulk of his ministry training a small group of future leaders rather than an army of foot soldiers. No doubt, he knew the future of the church, humanly speaking, depended upon the quality of its leadership.

Even if there weren't a biblical mandate to equip leaders to lead, the practical benefits would still make it a wise choice.

To begin with, training draws people together. Most church boards are made up of folks from widely divergent backgrounds. But a training program can provide everyone with common experiences and vocabulary, making communication easier.

It doesn't even matter whether everyone agrees with the content of the training. Just going through the process gives us a starting point from which to launch a discussion. It enables us to invest words, terms, and situations with an agreed-upon meaning. That way, even when we disagree, we at least understand one another's frame of reference well enough to intelligently discuss the differences.

Second, training is essential because a church is different from a business organization. It is spiritually centered and run by volunteers. It has a radically different bottom line: relationships. While some of the leadership principles of business carry over, many do not. A training program can help a board to recognize and respond to these differences.

Frankly, it strikes me as ironic that most board members receive so little training today, because the modern-day pastor receives so much. This is the age of continuing education. Additional degrees and further study are not only encouraged; in many cases, they are required. Few churches would settle for a pastor or staff member who lacked formal training.

But if the increasing complexities of ministry necessitate more training for the "professionals," don't they mean the same for the rest of the leadership team? And if I, as pastor, fail to train leaders to lead, what right do I have to complain about the way the board members do their job, or the decisions they make?

As valuable as training can be, if handled poorly, it can do more harm than good. That's why I once wrote an article for LEADERSHIP entitled, "Why Board Training Goes Awry." But if training is done right, it can contribute to a beautiful partnership between pastor and board. Here are some key points I've had to learn.

No Lobbying

One of the most important things to remember is the difference between training and lobbying. The two are easily confused.

Training presents information away from the pressure of an immediate decision. It's designed to change the way we think.

Lobbying presents information in the middle of the decision-making process. It's designed to change the way we vote.

I never fully grasped the difference until we were about to hire our first full-time associate. I had someone in mind, a member of the church who I knew would hit the ground running. I also know that every church growth expert agreed we should hire now, before the need became acute. That way we would be staffing for growth, not maintenance.

I figured it was an ideal time to teach the board the importance of staffing for growth and the advantages of hiring from within. So I put together a packet of all the literature I could find on the subject, sent it out, and asked everyone to be prepared to discuss it at our next meeting.

When we began our discussion, Jim spoke first. "Thanks for the helpful articles, Larry," he said. "But I know there is always another side to every issue. All these articles agree with you. I'd like to see some from the other side as well."

When I told him there weren't any, that all the experts agreed with me, he looked at me with disbelief. He thought I was lying. It took a long time to convince him otherwise.

I learned a valuable lesson that night. When information is presented in the middle of a decision-making process, most people will look on it as a lobbying effort, not training. Regardless how accurate or helpful the information might be, if it is presented too close to a vote, it will be treated with skepticism — an appropriate response to a lobbyist's presentation.

Yet many of us share the bulk of our insights when an issue is at hand. Until then, the principles we've gleaned from reading, conferences, and experience stay stored in our memory, notebooks, and files. When the board is faced with a tough decision, we pull them out and present them in an attempt to sway their decision. But by then, it is too late. What could have been helpful training comes across as nothing more than manipulative lobbying.

There is another important difference between lobbying and training. Training allows people the freedom and time to change their mind. Lobbying asks for a decision right now.

Most of us have had the experience of later championing an idea we initially rejected. But the change seldom occurs overnight. We need time to reflect and mull over an issue. When I tried to train our board members in the middle of the decision-making process, they had no time to reflect and change their mind. The pressure was on. But now, if they do their best thinking in the shower or on the way home, that's fine. They have the time to do so.

When John, one of our board members, was first exposed to the principles of church growth, he rejected them *a priori*. "Frankly, this stuff disturbs me," he said at the beginning of one meeting. "We're supposed to be a church, not a business. All these guys care about is numbers."

But with the passage of time and further exposure, he worked through his initial concerns. Now John is one of our board's strongest advocates for growth. More than once, he's pointed out an area where we were veering from a basic church growth principle.

But if John's first exposure to these principles had been during a major, growth-related decision, probably he would still be an opponent today. Lobbying would have forced him to digest the information quickly and make a decision. As part of the debating and decision-making process, he would have had to defend his position publicly. And unfortunately, once a person takes a public stand, he seldom changes his mind. It's too threatening to the ego.

Avoiding lobbying removes skepticism and allows people to buy into ideas based on the ideas' merit, not our pressure.

Flexibility

Another key to an effective training program is flexibility. For me, that means not being slavishly tied to a set curriculum.

Whenever I talk or write about training leaders, people ask me for a copy of the curriculum we use. They're always surprised when I say we have none. Rather than using a set body of material, I select topics of study as we go along, trying to match our training to forthcoming needs.

I realize a curriculum can save time, cover a subject in depth, and add a sense of authority to the things I'm trying to get across.

But once we've started a program, most of us want to stick to it. We then resist excursions down a side road. Yet taking a side road is exactly what I want the freedom to do. I want to deal with issues that soon will be hot and take advantage of teachable moments. Not that I wait until we're in the middle of making a decision (as we've seen, that would be lobbying, not training), but I tackle an issue the moment I see it looming on the horizon.

Say, for example, it's becoming obvious that our growth is going to make an additional service necessary within the next year. I want to be able to stop and study what other churches have done in that situation. And I want us to learn that now, well before we're forced to make our own decision.

A second reason why I haven't tried to develop a set curriculum is that I want to stress training as an ongoing process, not a one-time event. Most of us view a training course as something to be finished; once we've completed the material, we consider ourselves trained. That's the last thing I want our leadership team to think. We can't afford to stop learning and growing. To emphasize this, I've chosen to avoid a curriculum with a clearly defined start and end.

In short, it's not easy to be a church leader. The demands on our board constantly change, and new and unforeseen situations crop up. A flexible training program is the only way I can guarantee the board's training will relate to its task.

For instance, a few months ago we had to deal with a case of sexual immorality. What made it difficult was that the sinning brother acknowledged the sin, verbally repented, and put himself into an accountability relationship. But he continued to sin.

We'd never before had someone who repented and denounced a relationship, while at the same time had fallen back into it. As a board, we had to make a tough decision. Should we apply the discipline procedures found in 1 Corinthians 5, or keep trying to help this person turn around?

We stopped our current training topic and spent the next couple of sessions wrestling with church discipline, sexual purity, and corporate responsibility. Our study led us to a consensus that as church leaders we could judge people only by their ongoing actions, not their tears, so we asked him to leave the fellowship, which he angrily did. It was a classic teachable moment. I have no doubt that the Bible studies and lessons in that setting never will be forgotten. By keeping ourselves flexible, we were able to study what we needed to know when we needed to know it.

Repetition

Most training programs cover an item once and go on. We tend to think if we have carefully covered an issue once, everyone understands. We forget our own need to hear an idea several times before it soaks in. Also, we fear boring people, so we may move on long before the lesson has been learned.

To keep from doing that, I keep in mind the three stages of learning: exposure, familiarity, and understanding. A lesson hasn't been learned until we've completed the third stage.

The *exposure* stage is by far the most exciting. It's fun to be exposed to new ideas, to wrestle with concepts and principles for the first time. When suddenly I grasp what was only a mystery before, there is a sense of exhilaration.

During the second stage, *familiarity*, there are few surprises. I know where the discussion is going, so there is a great temptation to tune out because "I know this stuff already."

But actually, I don't.

Familiarity falls far short of the final stage of learning, *understanding*. When I'm familiar with a subject, I recognize where the teacher is going. When I understand a subject, I can teach and apply it myself. Only then has the lesson been learned.

Keeping these three stages in mind has helped me avoid the temptation to move on from an idea too early. For instance, we studied the principles of church growth on and off for about three years. If I had stopped after the first book or a couple of articles, we all would have had a nodding acquaintance with the subject. But we would not have been able to explain church growth to others in the congregation or base decisions on a mature understanding of it.

But even when we fully grasp a subject, it needs to be repeated within a couple of years. Otherwise, a turnover of even a few people can destroy the unified understanding of the board.

Obviously, going over the same material year after year could be a pain for those who have been on the board a long time. To save them the agony, we've put together a starter packet for new members. It covers material we feel every member needs in order to understand our board's organizational climate and way of thinking. Our current packet includes books like:

The Unity Factor, by Larry Osborne

Basic Principles of Policy Governance, by John Carver

Purpose Driven Church, by Rick Warren

Good to Great, by Jim Collins

Obviously the list changes over time to reflect our changing needs and what's easily available in the marketplace. But with this packet, new board members get a running start, and the gains of today aren't lost tomorrow.

Building Leaders

I once thought equipping the saints for ministry was limited to helping people develop godly character, a knowledge of the Bible, and a specific ministry skill. I left the job of equipping church leaders to the seminaries and Bible schools.

Now, for the sake of our church's long-range health, I've made equipping our leaders to lead a top priority. It has paid off in a board that consistently works through tough issues without losing its cool or its unity.

But the church has not been the only beneficiary. Our board members have benefited as well. The same principles that have made them better church leaders also have helped them lead at home and in the marketplace.

I remember when one elder called to tell me about a major promotion. He was moving into a management position and was going to be overseeing some significant projects. After I congratulated him, he said, "This is a new track for me, but I am excited about it. I've already seen a lot of areas where I can apply the things we've been learning about leadership. I'm confident I'll do a good job."

He has. And his company would be surprised to learn that part of the credit goes to the training he received as an elder in his church.

SEVEN

THE SHEPHERDING MEETING

A few board members obviously saw it as a second-string meeting, making it a low priority in their busy schedules. But within a year, our problems with absenteeism disappeared. These meetings had become the most important ones on our schedule.

W hen I entered the pastorate, I wasn't so naive as to expect board meetings to be the high point of my ministry. But I didn't expect them to be the low point, either.

Yet by the end of my first year, I couldn't think of anything less appealing. I was dismayed by our lack of trust and unity, ignorance of church growth principles, and inordinate time spent on trivial details.

Worse, we were neglecting the weightier things of leadership: extended prayer, seeking God's vision, brainstorming, dreaming, training, and developing unity.

Frustrated with our inability to find time to deal with these vital areas, I hit upon an idea. *Why not schedule an extra monthly meeting to deal with them exclusively?* I wasn't sure if the board would go for it, but they agreed to try the meetings for the rest of the year. So I put together a series of "shepherding meetings" to zero in on three areas: (1) team building, (2) training, and (3) prayer.

Initially, the shepherding meetings met with some passive resistance. Nobody said anything, but a few board members obviously saw it as a second-string meeting, making it a low priority in their busy schedules. Their attendance was sporadic at best. But within a year, our problems with absenteeism disappeared; these meetings had become the most important ones on our schedules. In fact, we made them a permanent fixture. Without them, much of our board's unity, trust, and efficiency would be lost.

Their beauty lies in the fact they give me a regularly scheduled forum for the essential building blocks for unity and effective leadership. I no longer have to try to jam training and prayer into an already packed agenda. Instead, I can relax, knowing I'm guaranteed at least one meeting a month devoted exclusively to them.

Not a Business Meeting

The secret of a successful shepherding meeting is to differentiate it as much as possible from a business meeting.

To keep the distinction sharp, we stay away from all forms of decision making. No votes are allowed, no minutes taken. This helps keep my attempts at training from coming off as lobbying. And it allows our discussion of key issues to be spared the posturing that an impending vote can bring.

We used to meet in the evening but found most board members didn't have the energy for lengthy discussions or extended prayer after a long day at work. So a few years ago we started meeting on a Saturday morning. We start fresh, and we've made a symbolic statement that team building, training, and prayer are worth one Saturday morning a month.

We begin with breakfast, usually in a home. While we eat, we swap stories, catch up on news, and renew our friendship.

Then we move into our training time. For about an hour, we'll discuss some aspect of ministry or church leadership. The session might be based on a reading assignment or an issue the church is currently facing. Depending on how much I know about the subject, and how much they know, I'll take on the role of a teacher, discussion leader, or fellow learner.

Lastly, in our role as shepherds of the flock, we pray for the sheep. Concerns, needs, and requests are shared, and we pray.

No, it's not like most board business meetings. But our intent is that it not be.

Team Building

Of my three goals for a shepherding meeting — team building, training, and prayer — team building is by far the easiest to accomplish. It's a natural by-product of our time together.

First, just spending extra time together builds unity. As we saw in chapter 2, when people increase the amount of time they spend together, there will be a corresponding increase in their regard and appreciation for one another.

It would be nice if unity in Christ guaranteed unity on the board. But human nature being what it is, most groups also need to spend significant time together in order to jell.

Second, the training segment provides everyone with common points of reference. Whether or not we all agree with the material, we all gain a common vocabulary and a set of shared experiences from which to draw.

Third, praying together promotes harmony. There is something about coming before our heavenly Father that dissipates spiritual sibling rivalries. It's hard to fight with a prayer partner.

This team building has had a significant impact on our business meetings. They've lost their confrontational edge. I can't remember the last time we had an honest-to-goodness argument. Not that we don't disagree, sometimes strongly. But we've found truth in the old saying, "Friends discuss; strangers argue."

Our meetings are shorter now, too. When our board members lacked trust in one another, they watched like hawks to make sure no one got away with anything. As a result, any request, be it for a music stand or office equipment, was greeted with suspicion and twenty questions.

But after a year of shepherding meetings, we were able to cut business meetings to a couple of hours. This happened despite our dealing with some sticky issues:

huge budget increases, a change in worship format, adding an additional service, and canning the Sunday evening service.

Absenteeism has also ceased to be a problem. It's no secret that people stay away from unpleasant things, and drawn-out, contentious meetings are not most folks' idea of a pleasant evening.

When morale goes up, so does participation. Just a few months ago, one board member showed up at a 7:30 A.M. meeting looking beat. He had arrived home from a business trip at 2:30 that morning. Surprised to see him, I asked, "Why aren't you in bed?"

"Because," he said, "I want to be here."

Training

For board training to be most effective, I've found, it needs to be (1) done in the context of ministry, and (2) highlighted as a significant priority. These two things are easily accomplished with shepherding meetings.

Consider the need for training to be done in the context of ministry. I used to think the best way to train board members was to do it before they joined the board. It was a grand idea. But for most pastors, it's simply not possible.

The board is already in place when they arrive. In most cases, it would take years to gain approval for, install, and train prospective board members. Add to that the high turnover rate of both pastors and lay people in an increasingly mobile society, and the only realistic option is on-the-job training.

But that's not so bad. Many experts believe on-the-job training is the best way to train leaders and managers.[1] It offers significant advantages: a greater hunger in the learners, immediate application, and a quicker learning curve. More important, those in the trenches distinguish between the important and the esoteric. They know what's significant and what isn't.

I noticed, when I was a seminary student, that there were always two sets of questions asked in class: those asked by students already serving in ministry, and those asked by students preparing for ministry. Those in the trenches weren't too concerned about the differences between infralapsarianism, supralapsarianism, and a labrador retriever. Those yet to taste battle often thought it was the most important question in the world.

That's why, given the choice, I'll always choose an on-the-job training program over one for prospective board members. Leadership is not an academic subject, but an art and a skill. It can best be learned in a hands-on environment where the lessons and principles can quickly be put to the test.

I've found that no matter what subject we are studying — group dynamics, the optimum staff/member ratio, how to pray for the sick, or how to lead a small group Bible study — the board members want to know, "How does this work in real life?" Because they're already on the job, they know what's practical and what's not. If it isn't, they don't want to waste any more time on the subject.

The second advantage to using our shepherding meetings for training: It highlights training as a significant priority, an event worthy of its own forum.

When I started training board members, I simply tacked training onto the beginning of another meeting. The result: no one took it seriously. Assignments were incomplete and attention halfhearted.

But once we set aside a time and place just for training, people brought their books and articles marked, and their assignments completed. Instead of viewing training as a preliminary to the real meeting, or a veiled attempt at lobbying, they saw it as a significant event.

A number of years ago, I conducted a survey of pastors to find out how many were actively training their boards and what the results were. Many pastors claimed to have a training program, but to ensure they did, I asked for a description of what they were doing. Those who were actively training their boards were then listed as "training pastors."

My next step was to contact the board members in the churches of these training pastors. I asked them, "Do you receive any training for church leadership or board membership?"

To my surprise, many said no.

I couldn't figure it out. Their pastors had described in detail the training. Now these same board members were telling me they hadn't been trained at all.

As I puzzled over the conflicting answers, I noticed something interesting. Among the board members who were being trained but claimed they weren't, the pastor was nearly always doing his training at the beginning of a business meeting. Apparently, this caused some board members to view it as an insignificant preliminary to the real meeting. So they tuned out, much as people do during the perfunctory prayers and devotions at the beginning of a meeting.

One thing I seldom emphasize during our training sessions is personal spiritual growth. That surprises a lot of people.

But I have my reasons. To begin with, our board members have proven themselves to be spiritually mature; that's a requirement for selection. Not that they've arrived spiritually or become finished theologians, but they do represent the cream of our crop spiritually.

The last thing most of them need is another Bible study or devotional pep talk. They get plenty of that from our Sunday messages and home Bible studies, and their devotional life. What they need is a knowledge and understanding of the local church — how it works, what causes it to grow, and how to keep it healthy.

That doesn't mean I consider spiritual growth to be unimportant. I don't. It's vital, particularly for leaders. And I find it scandalous to hear people refer to their experience on a church board as a spiritual low point. Serving on the board should cause someone's spiritual life to flourish, not wane.

But the solution is not necessarily more Bible studies. The solution is a careful selection process, removal of the forms and structures that undercut unity, and adequate training.

For maximum impact, it seems, board training requires a distinct, highlighted time and place. For our purposes, one Saturday morning each month provides that.

Prayer

Our shepherding meetings also provide an unhurried time for extended prayer.

Until we started these meetings, I tried to fit prayer into the beginning of a business meeting. It was a big deal if we spent five minutes praying; ten minutes was a revival. Most often, we simply replaced it with prayer's popular substitute: an "opening word" of prayer.

But once we set aside a special time and place for prayer, there was no longer a subtle pressure to rush, and we stopped worrying about dragging out an already long meeting. Our actions also began to more clearly mirror our rhetoric. We all agreed that prayer was important, even necessary for effective spiritual leadership. But we didn't pray, as long as prayer remained a preliminary to our meetings rather than the reason for them.

When we gather to pray, we follow some basic guidelines.

First, we limit the time spent sharing requests. It's too easy to spend thirty minutes talking about what to pray for and ten minutes praying. So most requests are brought up as we pray. If something needs an explanation, it's included in the prayer. If a person needs clarification, he interrupts and asks for it.

Second, we pray conversationally, with each person praying for no more than one item at a time. This keeps long-winded prayer warriors from putting everyone else to sleep.

Third, we pray for individuals by name, and we pray specifically. Group prayer can be awfully generic: "Lord, guide John in the big decision he has to make;

take care of Carol's unspoken request." In my book, powerful prayer is specific prayer.

Finally, we pray candidly. If our board is going to make a difference, we have to be candid with God and one another. I ask our board members to pray for anyone whom they see in need of God's help. I don't care if their perception of a need is based on a rumor, an intuition, or hard facts. I'd rather find out we prayed for a false alarm than fail to pray for people because their need hasn't become acute enough to be public knowledge. We need to be praying for a struggling marriage at the first sign of trouble. It does no good to wait until a separation or divorce confirms what we earlier sensed in our spirits. By then it's too late.

Obviously, with this candor, the door to gossip and slander is wide open. I would not recommend this approach for a large group prayer meeting or a spiritually immature board. But once a level of unity, trust, and maturity has been built into a leadership team, I wouldn't do without it. So far, we've never been burned by gossip. But if someone does slip, we'll deal with the situation biblically and forcefully. In the meantime, I'll keep urging our board to pray candidly and freely. I'll gladly take the risks that go with doing so. After all, prayer is a form of spiritual warfare. I'm not sure it was ever meant to be tame or safe.

God expects the leaders of his church to pray. Shepherding meetings have helped us to more faithfully fulfill that responsibility.

EIGHT

WHAT DOES THE BOARD NEED TO KNOW?

Some of the keys to developing a healthy church run counter to conventional wisdom and common practice. I call them the paradoxes of ministry. On the surface they appear to be all wrong, but in real life they work, resulting in faster growing, healthier, and stronger churches. It's precisely this sort of principle I want to get across to the board. The paradoxes hold the key to our effectiveness as a leadership team.

Jim wasn't too surprised when I asked if we could meet together for a few weeks. A sharp, young Christian, he assumed I wanted to recruit him for some area of ministry or disciple him for future leadership. But he was wrong. I didn't want to recruit or train him for anything. I wanted him to train me.

A successful, fast-rising copywriter for a local advertising firm, Jim was an expert in the art of persuasion. I hoped his insights into people and motivation could help me in my ministry. He agreed to help me find out.

For the next few weeks, we met at a local restaurant, and I took notes as he unfolded the basic principles behind modern advertising. When we came to his area of expertise, direct mail, I was dumbfounded. Almost all of his advice ran directly counter to what I considered to be good common sense.

For instance, he showed me that longer letters were more likely to be read than shorter ones; that a casual, conversational tone far outsold a polished, literary style; that a P.S. was the most important part of any letter; and that script-style typeface, while it might look nice, was a guaranteed way to keep people from reading my correspondence.

I was surprised and embarrassed. Most of my previous congregational letters had been short, polished, void of a P.S., and printed in fancy script so they would "look nice."

My lessons with Jim not only taught me how to become a better persuader; they also sensitized me to how often the seemingly obvious thing to do is the wrong thing to do. It's true not only in advertising, but also in nearly every field, including ministry.

Like Jim's principles for successful advertising, some of the keys to developing a healthy church run counter to conventional wisdom and common practice. I call them the paradoxes of ministry. On the surface they appear all wrong, but in real life they work, resulting in faster growing, healthier, and stronger churches.

It's precisely this sort of principle I want to get across during our shepherding meetings. The paradoxes hold the key to our effectiveness as a leadership team. In this chapter and the next, I'll offer seven of the most important concepts I try to teach our board members — beginning with three paradoxes they've found surprising and significant.

Ignore Your Weaknesses

The usual pattern for planning in churches goes something like this:

1. Size up the ministry.
2. Identify any major weaknesses.
3. Develop and implement a plan for removing those weaknesses.

While this might sound like a great approach, in reality it seldom does much good. In many cases, it actually undercuts the strengths that already exist. It violates one of the most important paradoxes of church leadership: Strong churches ignore their weaknesses.

Not that these churches are unaware of problems or blinded to flaws. On the contrary, they are usually aware of problems and quick to act. But at the same time, they have learned to ignore weaknesses in favor of focusing on strengths. Instead of worrying about all the things the church or pastor does poorly, they identify and build upon those things the church or pastor does well. They know it is easier and more effective to build upon strength than to build around weakness.

When we spend time worrying about weaknesses, there is seldom enough time or energy left to identify and develop strengths. Instead of creative and assertive, we end up defensive. The result is most often a mediocre program, designed more to minimize weaknesses than to capitalize on opportunities.

I think of one church that, frozen out by the high cost of New England real estate, was forced to meet in inadequate facilities for ten years. Trying to overcome this weakness, the pastor and board members spent great amounts of time, money, and emotional energy attempting to come up with a better facility. Unfortunately, they couldn't find one. And in the meantime, they failed to develop and build upon the two greatest strengths they had.

First, they were blessed with a host of young, open-minded families, willing and often eager to try new things (as evidenced by their attendance at a church that met in a shopping center). Many new and innovative programs that would take years to launch in a more traditional setting would have been quickly accepted by these folks.

But because the leaders channeled most of their creative energy into land-search committees and fund raising, they didn't have the energy or creativity to develop new and innovative ministries. Instead, they settled for a traditional style of ministry. Ironically, it was a style that needed excellent facilities in order to succeed.

Second, the absence of a large mortgage left them in excellent financial shape. Most years, they ended up well in the black. They had the money to hire top-quality staff capable of designing and leading an outstanding program.

Yet most of this money was stashed in a building fund. Instead of a top-notch staff, they settled for an excellent senior pastor and a group of poorly paid, part-time assistants. The result? Inadequate staffing to go along with their inadequate facilities.

It's no wonder that after a fast start this church began to slow down, and then started moving backward. Its leaders had fallen into the trap of problem-centered planning, a common occurrence for those who focus on their weaknesses.

Instead of being problem-centered, strong churches tend to be potential-centered. They don't ask, "What are we doing wrong?" They ask, "What are we doing uncommonly well? What things attracted the people we now have, and what has kept them coming back? How can we do these things better? How can we strengthen our strengths?"

One church in our area has a strong ministry to senior adults. Any visitor is sure to be struck by the preponderance of gray and balding heads — and the lack of empty seats. At the same time, it's hard not to notice the one glaring weakness: the absence of young families.

Problem-centered planning would suggest that the leaders of this church search for ways to bring in young families. A younger pastor, a few choruses instead of hymns, and three or four youthful board members might be good places to start.

But in reality, trying to solve the young-families weakness would be a big mistake. Such changes would alienate, to some degree, many of the older saints they have. And if the changes were carried out gently enough so as not to ruffle any feathers, they probably wouldn't draw the young families they were designed to attract. In place of a dynamic ministry to seniors (tailored to their tastes, interests, and needs), the church would likely be left with a diluted ministry satisfying neither the older saints nor the younger ones.

Potential-centered planning, on the other hand, would suggest hiring another older pastor, repairing the organ, increasing daytime ministries, and developing a stronger visitation and support system. Instead of worrying about weaknesses, the church would capitalize on its greatest strength: an effective ministry to senior adults.

When it came time for our church to add our first full-time associate, most people assumed we would have him concentrate on our weakest area of ministry: a fledgling youth ministry that averaged only five kids per week. Instead, we called him with the express stipulation that he spend no time with our struggling youth program. Rather, we asked Mike to focus on our two greatest strengths: ministry to adults and young children. As he focused on these, our ministry continued to grow in both health and numbers. Soon we had the people and financial resources to support a top-quality youth program. Then we brought on a staff person to develop one.

Every church has its areas of weakness, but the churches that accomplish the most have learned not to worry about them. They've accepted the fact that great strengths come with correspondingly great weaknesses. They know that no one church can do the work of the entire kingdom; churches, like individuals, have been gifted and called to do some things uncommonly well and others not at all. They've grasped the first and perhaps most important paradox of successful leadership: Ignore your weaknesses.

Let Squeaky Wheels Squeak

Weaknesses are not the only thing to be ignored. There are also certain people who are best treated with benign neglect. I call these folks "squeaky wheels."

They are found within every church, sometimes on the fringe, other times in the leadership. Unlike other members with legitimate complaints and criticisms, genuine squeaky wheels (1) are never quite happy with the direction of ministry and (2) let everybody know it.

The natural response is to oil these squeaky wheels. We alter our plans or give them extra attention in the hope of silencing their criticism. Unfortunately, it seldom works. Most squeaky wheels keep right on squeaking, for a simple reason: they don't squeak for a lack of oil; they squeak because it's their nature to squeak. Wise church leaders know an important paradox: Church harmony is inversely related to the amount of time spent oiling squeaky wheels.

This is a lesson the church board and I were slow to grasp. In our zeal for maintaining peace and unity within the body, we often allowed a small group of chronic complainers to have an inordinate impact upon our decisions and ministry. In effect, we gave them veto power over anything we suggested, or might suggest.

A man I'll call Fred was one such squeaky wheel. Whether it was our song selection, a program change, my preaching content, or a rumor of someone else's dissatisfaction, something was always wrong. If we didn't hear about it directly, we heard about it secondhand. For nearly three years, we tried everything we could think of to keep him happy.

Nothing worked, but we kept on trying because we feared losing him. We were a small, struggling congregation, and Fred was an excellent musician and our only pianist. We felt we needed him desperately. We also feared his influence. Even though his moodiness was legend, most people in the congregation genuinely cared for him. Over the years, he and his wife had helped a number of couples through rough waters. His music had ministered to many. So we feared how people would react if he got too upset, or if, heaven forbid, he left the church. Would they leave, too?

We assumed it was possible to keep everyone happy. We failed to realize that some people (studies show as high as 7 to 10 percent) will be unhappy no matter what. Finally, in the middle of a discussion of how to handle Fred's latest grievance, Bob, a board member, asked why I didn't just take him up on it next time he threatened to resign. To my surprise, the rest of the board chimed in with their agreement.

So I did. And sure enough, Fred and his wife soon left the church. But the musical crisis we dreaded never materialized. We found someone else of equal talent within a week. As for his influence, that was overblown. No one else left the church, and only four or five people even mentioned his departure. As for disunity, those days of trying to walk on egg shells were the least unified days we've known.

The fact is, oiling squeaky wheels can be hazardous to the health of a church. Leaders who place too much emphasis on keeping everyone happy risk abdicating leadership. Instead of initiating, we end up reacting.

"What does God want us to do?" is replaced with, "What do they want us to do?" Without realizing it, we grant a small core of chronic complainers an invisible but powerful position on our leadership team.

Giving too much attention to a few squeaky wheels also sends an unspoken message to the congregation: The best way to have an influence is to complain, and the louder and more often you complain, the better. No wonder, then, that leaders who try to oil every squeaky wheel have the most wheels to oil.

Another problem with giving too much attention to squeaky wheels is that it can cause us to neglect those who are happily carrying on the ministry of the church. A common rule of thumb, The 80/20 Rule, states that 80 percent of a leader's time will be spent dealing with 20 percent of the people. If so, it behooves church leaders to ask, "Which 20 percent of the people are getting 80 percent of our time and attention? Is it the complainers or the producers?"

In the past, the board and I would have had to answer, "The complainers." But now that we've learned the importance of letting squeaky wheels squeak, we no longer face every decision with nagging questions about how "they" will react. And I no longer lie awake at night figuring ways to keep everybody happy. Instead, we've learned to relax and let our squeaky wheels go right on squeaking.

Make Fuzzy Plans

The third paradox applies to our plans. The common assumption is that the best-run churches have the clearest and most detailed blueprint for the future.

But more often the best-run churches make "fuzzy plans." Not that they neglect planning, but they avoid making plans that are too rigid or detailed. They make plans that give general direction without committing anyone to an irrevocable course of action.

There is a place for detailed strategies and precise plans, but as a rule the best plans are flexible and easily changed. This is particularly true in two areas — finances and operational policy. Ironically, both are often the recipient of our most detailed and inflexible planning.

Take finances. Many churches opt for a highly detailed and restrictive annual budget. The planning process is drawn out and intense. Then once the budget is adopted, it can't be changed until the next year.

While the motivation for such a process (a desire to avoid fiscal irresponsibility) is excellent, the cure can be worse than the disease. The way most churches devise a budget, the process begins months before it goes into effect. That means the final months of a budget year are planned up to fifteen months ahead of time, despite the fact there is no way to accurately forecast income and expenditures that far in advance. Then, because the figures are considered inflexible, no matter what needs or opportunities come up, the answer is, "Sorry, it's not in the budget; wait until next year."

In contrast, we've opted for fuzzy budget planning. Though our budget is clear and detailed, it is also flexible enough to allow for midstream changes. We don't view it as a rigid ceiling on our expenditures; we look at it as an educated (and somewhat hazy) guess of our income and expenses in the coming year. It's a guide, not a straitjacket.

That way, if something breaks, we can fix it. When badly needed office equipment becomes available at a good price, we can buy it. The only requirements are that (1) we have the money (we never spend more than we have), and (2) our elder board approves the expenditure. The result: a ministry freed to move ahead rather than stalled until next year.

Those who might have resisted a fuzzy budget have had their objections preempted by two steps we've taken. First, we have committed ourselves to never spend more than we have. That way, our flexibility can't bankrupt the church. Second, we tell everyone that the budget is only a planning tool. As long as we make that clear, no one objects when unforeseen changes cause us to overspend some area of the budget.

A second area where fuzziness can be helpful is in the realm of church policy. Most church constitutions and policy statements are too detailed and restrictive. They remind me of a complaint an old Navy man made: "Every time a sailor drowns, a new regulation is passed."

Our motives are usually noble. We want to make sure the church stays true to its original purpose. So to protect future members from inept or evil leaders, we lay down regulations. But too often they tie the hands of future leaders, stripping them of the flexibility they need to cope with changing circumstances.

For instance, one key to the health of our church has been a strong home fellowship ministry. These weekly home Bible studies are attended by over 70 percent of our adults. Yet we never could have started them if our constitution had institutionalized the traditional midweek meeting at the church. Instead of having the freedom to develop an alternative format for study and prayer, we would have been forced to keep an old one alive, even though it no longer met the needs of our people.

Rigid plans, guidelines, and regulations work fine in a stable environment. But if there is anything we know about the future, it's that it won't be like today. It will have new problems, needs, and opportunities, and new leaders as well. Those leaders will need the freedom to lead. So why limit their options? Why hinder the Spirit's ability to replace our favorite wineskins with new ones we've never thought of?

Planning is vital, but by purposely keeping plans fuzzy, we can give future leaders a track to run on without forcing them to respond in ways that no longer fit a changing situation.

NINE

WHAT ELSE DOES THE BOARD NEED TO KNOW?

Unless we are challenged to act differently, most of us will try to solve today's problems with yesterday's solutions.

T he paradoxes in chapter 8 aren't the only things a board member needs to know, of course. Unfortunately, we can't cover all the important principles within this book. But I believe four more are worthy of special mention. Each has had a major impact upon our ministry, and, like the paradoxes in the previous chapter, runs counter to the way most board members think when they join our board.

Form Follows Function

The first principle I'll mention is so important that I cover it on the first night of my pastor's class for people new to the church. I want everyone in the congregation to understand that when it comes to designing a ministry, form must follow function.

"Form follows function" is an architectural principle. Simply put, it means the design of a building should be dictated by its intended use. Applied to the church, it suggests we first decide what we want to accomplish and then design our programs and ministries accordingly.

While that may seem painfully obvious, it's ignored all the time. I think of one church that had more than a thousand people attending morning worship. But on Wednesday night, the church was lucky if twenty showed up. So the pastor asked for permission to start midweek home Bible studies as a good way to get more people involved in weekly study and prayer. The board turned him down. "We have enough problems getting people to come out on Wednesday night," they said, "without adding any unnecessary competition."

Too often, maintaining a form (in this case, Wednesday night study at the church) becomes more important than its original function (weekly study and prayer). Over the long haul, maintaining forms without considering the underlying functions produces a staid and traditional ministry resistant to innovation.

Something in our human nature causes us to stick with the familiar and comfortable. Unless we are challenged to act differently, most of us try to solve today's problems with yesterday's solutions. That's fine as long as they work. But when they don't, it's time for a change.

The first step in designing a function-oriented ministry is to decide what we're trying to accomplish. In our case, we've settled on four functions as essential in a healthy ministry:

1. The study and practical application of God's Word

2. The experience of meaningful worship

3. The development of significant and supportive relationships

4. The expansion of God's kingdom.

We call them our Four Ws: The Word, worship, warmth, and witness.

We judge every program by its ability to help us fulfill one, or at the most two, of these functions. That way, we're able to decide what we should and should not do. It doesn't matter if every other church our size or stripe has a particular program — or even that it has worked for us in the past. If it won't help us more effectively fulfill one of these functions, we won't do it. And similarly, we won't reject an idea just because no one else has tried it. If it holds the promise of helping us do a better job with one of the functions, we'll give it a try.

For instance, at this time, we've decided not to have a choir. Occasionally, that's a cause of concern to visitors who have a hard time imagining a "real church" without one. But in our case, instead of helping us fulfill our primary functions, a choir actually would set us back. It would cut into our congregational singing, something that has proven to be our most effective tool for fostering meaningful praise and worship. And a choir would undermine our home fellowships, a ministry that involves 70 percent of our adults on a weekly basis, helping them to build relationships and probe deeper into God's Word. Experience has shown us that most of those involved in a weekly choir practice would not have the time to continue in a home fellowship.

So, even though there are many good reasons to have a choir, we've chosen not to have one. Maybe we will someday. But if we do, it will be because we've decided that a choir could help us more effectively accomplish our primary goals, not because every other church has one.

Let Dying Programs Die

Another principle board members need to know in order to be effective: Let dying programs die, and put those that are terminally ill out of their misery.

A number of years ago I was called to consult with a small suburban church. The pastor was overwhelmed, and the board discouraged, by what they saw as spiritual apathy. They were particularly concerned by their chronic lack of enough volunteers to carry on the weekly ministries.

At one point I asked the pastor to list every program and volunteer position in the church. His list had more positions to fill than the church had attenders on a typical Sunday morning. No wonder they couldn't find enough willing recruits! Their problem was not a spiritually lethargic congregation; it was a proliferation of programs far beyond their ability to sustain.

How had it happened? For years the board had failed to prune a single program. Every new ministry became a permanent fixture. Eventually the church began to drown in a sea of propped-up programs, traditions, and outdated ministries.

They had neglected what Peter Drucker calls one of the first steps to healthy organizational growth: "controlled abandonment."[1] But cutting our losses is easier said than done. Few of us are anxious to admit our mistakes, and human nature rings eternally optimistic. So when a program or ministry fails to live up to its expectations, we tend to hang on. No one wants to preside over the death of a once-thriving area of ministry. That sounds too much like failure or spiritual retreat.

Another thing that makes it hard to let a dying program die is that every program has its champions. Usually, they're former leaders who invested time and energy into making it successful during the good old days, or folks who once were especially ministered to by the program. For obvious reasons, they object when we start talking about pulling the plug. But we can't let that dissuade us, or we'll soon end up like my friend's church, so loaded with yesterday that we have no energy or resources left for today.

In our early years we included a time during our morning worship service for people to share prayer requests and praises. For years it worked well. It fostered community and helped us keep in touch.

But as the church grew, the size of the congregation became intimidating to many who wanted to speak up. Eventually, the only people sharing were extroverts. And their requests became increasingly less personal, most falling into the Please-pray-for-my-uncle's-best-friend-who's-dying-of-cancer category.

That created a dilemma. The sharing time was no longer effective, but it had been part of our services long enough to become a sacred tradition. There was no way we could finish it off with a sledge hammer. We had to use the next best thing: benign neglect.

We began by periodically "neglecting" to include the sharing time in our services. We also let it slide whenever we had Communion, a baptism, or a baby dedication. All the while, we kept our ear to the ground. If we heard some grumbling, we'd go back to sharing for a couple of weeks. If not, we'd "neglect" the sharing time again. Within five months it was a dead issue.

Wise board members know they have only a limited supply of time, energy and money. Periodically, they stop and ask, "Why are we doing this?" And if there is no good reason, they refuse to let their resources be wasted on outdated and ineffective programs. Sometimes that means having the courage to give a once-popular ministry a Christian burial.

Volunteers Aren't Cheap

A third thing board members need to understand is that it costs money to run an effective volunteer organization. Volunteers aren't cheap.

Like all churches, we use volunteers extensively. They run the bulk of our ministry, including many areas that traditionally have been turned over to paid staff. For instance, our church office has been run entirely by volunteers for a number of years. Only recently did we hire someone to work in the office, and even then it wasn't a secretary or receptionist. We hired an office administrator to recruit, train, and oversee the volunteer secretaries.

We've been blessed with a congregation that is willing to serve. At last count, something like 75 percent of our people had an identifiable area of service. I believe one of the main reasons we've been able to keep people involved is that our board has been willing to spend money on volunteers. They've rightly understood that the cost of keeping a volunteer happy and well equipped is not so much an expenditure as an investment.

Volunteers have the power to make or break our ministry. If they're plagued by poor morale or constant turnover, or if they lack the equipment and supplies they need, they won't be able to succeed. And any time they fail, we fail, too.

To keep our volunteers successful and motivated, we've loosened the purse strings to do three important things:

• *Purchase, as soon as possible, the equipment volunteers need.* When a teacher says he needs a new blackboard, we get it. When our musicians need another monitor, we buy it. And when the tape ministry gets bogged down, those who run the program get the additional duplicator or faster machine they need.

Occasionally, we have to ask for time to raise the money. But we try never to tell volunteers, "Sorry, you'll have to make do." Eventually, they know, they'll get what they need. And as long as they know that's true, they'll keep plugging away.

• *Cover the personal costs that volunteers incur.* Volunteering is enough of a sacrifice without asking people to bear the additional expense of child care, training, supplies, or mileage. So we reimburse our volunteers for costs they incur.

Included is the cost of any training they need in order to do their job better. When some of our office workers asked to take a computer class, we gladly picked up the tab. When the sound-booth crew signed up for an audio class at the local college, we paid their way. The same for a Sunday school coordinator who felt the need to take a C. E. class at a nearby seminary.

Not everyone takes advantage of this offer. In fact many people would rather pay their way and save us the money. But what's important is that the offer has been made. It lets our volunteers know we appreciate their sacrifice and we're trying to do everything we can to make their job easier.

• *Hire people for "suicide missions."* Suicide missions are easy to identify. They're the jobs and tasks with the highest turnover rates.

I once heard a business consultant say that any time three people fail in the same job, you can be sure the problem is with the job, not the people. That's an important point to keep in mind when dealing with volunteers. If a task burns out a succession of volunteers, the problem is with the job, not the volunteers. It's time to break the job into smaller parts or make it a paid position.

We've found that some jobs are simply unfair to ask a volunteer to do. They go far beyond the call of duty. Not that we can't find people to do them. Guilt and arm twisting work wonders. But at what price? The people who step forward to tackle these impossible jobs are usually our most loyal and hard-working volunteers.

That's why they step forward when no one else will. Allowing them to be eliminated by a suicide mission makes no sense. We need to keep these people for the long haul. So when faced with a suicide mission, we try hard to hire someone to do it.

Our Sunday morning set-up crew is a case in point. Because we meet in a shared facility, setting up and taking down our equipment is a major hassle. We used to have a crew of volunteers do the work. But as the church grew, the job became increasingly burdensome. The volunteers had to arrive early and leave late, and they had no time to talk with friends. Most were unable to enjoy the simple pleasure of coming to church with their family.

Once we saw what the task entailed, we decided it was too much to expect of volunteers on a weekly basis. So we hired some students. The job was just as hard, but now we had people who wanted to do it. Instead of feeling frustrated and used, the new set-up crew was happy for the job. And our volunteers were freed up for other tasks that were more appropriate for volunteer service.

A great general understands the importance of keeping front-line troops happy and well equipped. Along with setting a strategy for battle, that's his most important job. In a similar vein, church leaders need to keep their volunteer troops motivated and well supplied.

Even if the funds are low, much can be done. A gift subscription to a helpful magazine or a partial scholarship to a class or seminar can go a long way. If a board doesn't have the money to send key leaders to a conference, the tapes usually can be bought for a nominal price. More important than how much we actually spend is our attitude. Wise leaders are as generous as they can be toward their volunteers. They've come to grips with the fact that maintaining an effective army of volunteers isn't cheap.

Churches Don't Just Grow; They Change

A final principle I want everyone on our board to understand is that growing churches don't become just bigger versions of their past self. They change into something completely different.

Lyle Schaller has written the best material on this subject, particularly in *Looking in the Mirror*.[2] His insights have been so helpful that we ask every new board member to read the book, and we review the principles once or twice a year. As Schaller points out, a growing church doesn't just get bigger; it goes through a metamorphosis. At each stage the sociological pressures and expectations are radically different, so much so that a Baptist church of 250 usually will have more in common with a Pentecostal church of 250 than with another Baptist church of 500.

I was unaware of this principle when I came to the church. My ignorance nearly cost me my ministry.

Having spent my entire Christian life and ministry in larger churches (the smallest being around 900) I was suddenly thrust into a small church. I immediately tried to set up a big-church style: I took a strong leadership stance, spent thirty hours a week preparing sermons, and tried to upgrade the quality of everything from our newsletter to our worship services. In short, I tried to make our church a miniature version of the church I hoped it would be someday.

But that's not what our people wanted. Had they wanted the polish and wide range of programs offered by a larger church, they would have gone to one. What they were seeking was a warm and loving church family in which they could be known and cared for. It didn't matter to them if Aunt Martha was a little off key during her solo, the newsletter had a typo, or I failed to parse every verb in the text.

For three years I tried to make the strategies I'd learned in larger churches work. At the end of those three years, our average weekly attendance had increased by just a few percentage points. We'd become a revolving door, losing folks as fast as we gained new ones. Only after I began to adjust my style of leadership to more closely fit what people wanted and expected in a church our size did we grow.

But that created new problems. Each time we popped through one of the so-called attendance plateaus, we became a different kind of church, with new strengths, weaknesses, and expectations from our people. And that in turn called for new strategies.

Unfortunately, many, if not most, lay leaders assume (as I did) that all churches are basically alike — some are bigger than others, but what works for one will work for all.

As a consequence, we may pick the wrong models to emulate. I think of a church in the Northwest started by two hundred people from a large church on the other side of town. It was modeled after the mother church: same constitution, policies, programs, and ministries. But the church never experienced the same success.

Why? Because the style of ministry they brought with them was designed for a huge regional church, not a small community fellowship. Having evolved over fifteen years, the style was perfectly fitted to the mother church. But it had little to offer a struggling new church.

There is another consequence of failing to grasp this principle: needless alarm and frustration over changes that are nothing more than the natural results of growth. For instance, as a church grows, it loses much of its close-knit family feel. There is no way a group of 500 can experience the same community that a church of 150 enjoys. A larger church will also have less tolerance for shoddy programs and performance. In a church of 800, Aunt Martha's renditions aren't quaint; they're painful. It's not that people suddenly have become less loving. It's that the majority don't know her personally. So instead of appreciating her sincerity and effort, they're embarrassed by her mistakes.

Church government also goes through significant changes each time a church reaches a new plateau. In smaller churches a highly participatory form of congregational government usually works fine, but in a larger church it quickly becomes unwieldy. In most cases, the larger the church, the harder it is to get a quorum for a special business meeting. And contrary to what many people think, the problem is not apathy; it's changing sociological expectations. The larger the group, the more people look to their designated leaders for direction and decision making, and the less interest they have in the nuts and bolts of running the church.

Wise leaders understand and accept such changes as sociological facts of life. Rather than trying to turn back the clock, they adapt their methods. They recognize that churches don't just grow; they change.

PART III
COMMUNICATION

T E N

CHANGE DIPLOMACY

Christians aren't the only ones who respond negatively to change. It is a phenomenon found among all groups; it's more of a sociological problem than a spiritual problem. While that dashed my dreams of change without conflict, it didn't mean all was lost. There were still plenty of ways to limit the conflict and resistance that change can bring.

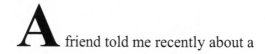 friend told me recently about a new church his denomination tried to start in a small mid-western town. The church got off to a great start. Then one Sunday, early in the second year, people arrived to find their old, hand-me-down pews replaced by padded stacking chairs, a surprise gift from an anonymous donor.

While everyone filed into the building, the pastor stood by the door beaming. He knew the congregation would be thrilled with the change, and he wanted to watch people's expressions as they came in.

Unfortunately, they weren't thrilled. They were surprised, startled, and upset. Within a few weeks, half of the congregation had left to form another church — one where they could worship God as he commanded, in pews rather than chairs.

His story reminded me of an old farmer's advice. "Go slow," he said. "Churches are a lot like horses. They don't like to be startled or surprised. It causes deviant behavior."

He was right. The fiercest battles in our churches are seldom fought over theology. More often, they are fought over change, sometimes even the slightest change.

I remember well a phone call I received, not long after my arrival at North Coast, from a key lay leader. He said his family was leaving the church, upset over all the changes I was making.

When I asked for specifics, I found I had committed two unpardonable sins. I had failed to schedule a third annual "All-Church New Year's Eve Party," and I had stopped using a closing hymn in our services. I hadn't thought of either change as significant. They both happened more by accident than design. But for some reason, they startled and surprised my caller. His "deviant behavior" was just what the old farmer had predicted.

There was a time when such petty and negative responses to change left me feeling angry and cynical. I wondered what it was about Christians that caused us to react so antagonistically to change. But after studying organizational culture, I came to realize that Christians aren't the only ones who respond negatively to change. It is a phenomenon found among all groups; it's more of a sociological problem than a spiritual problem.

While that dashed my dreams of change without conflict, it didn't mean all was lost. There were still plenty of ways to limit the conflict and resistance that change can bring. In particular, I've found that following a four-step process when introducing change significantly reduces the opposition and instances of deviant behavior. I use this process whenever I propose a change to the board, and our board uses it whenever we bring a new idea to the congregation. Here are the steps.

Step 1: Test the Waters

The first thing I do with a new idea is try to find out how people will react should the change actually take place.

Our government leaders are masters at this. Long before making a major proposal, they leak a rough sketch of the idea. Then they stand back and analyze the evening news reports and the response of their constituents. Was the idea vehemently rejected? Widely praised? Which points did opponents attack? Which criticisms were legitimate, and which were obviously partisan? And most important, what changes are needed before making the proposal official?

I follow the same course. I start by asking a cross section of our people — board members, unofficial power brokers, and the average man or woman in the pew — what they think of a possible change. For instance, I might ask their opinion of moving across town, adding a new staff member, or redesigning the church logo. Whether the change is major or insignificant, I try to get a reading on their reaction.

I've found it's best to ask in small, informal social settings. Larger groups tend to inhibit candor, and a formal setting or full-blown presentation causes most people to assume I'm asking for their approval rather than their opinion. At this stage, I'm not looking for approval. I'm not trying to gather a coalition or a support base. All I want is a reading on their initial reaction to the basic idea.

Testing the waters provides me with invaluable information. First, it lets me know if my dissatisfaction with the status quo is shared by others. If not, it's time to slow down and help other people to see the need. Either that or face deviant behavior from those who don't yet agree the changes are needed.

Second, testing the waters tells me what changes not to make. For instance, when our church was founded, it was named for the city we met in. When we moved to a nearby city, everyone agreed the name had to be changed. A number of us also wanted to drop the denominational tag, replacing it with a postscript stating our affiliation. We felt the tag was more of a hindrance than an asset, since most people on the West Coast have no idea what *Evangelical Free Church* represents. Despite the fact that Chuck Swindoll's ministry is just one hundred miles up the road, to this day I'm asked if we are a cult, a new religion, Pentecostals, fundamentalists, or we simply don't take offerings!

Most people seemed to like the idea of dropping the denominational label. But while testing the waters I discovered some strong opposition by a couple of key lay leaders, enough to create a major conflict. We dropped the idea. A test of the waters had shown us the price we would have to pay for making the change. It was a price we were unwilling to pay.

Third, testing the waters tells me which aspects of a proposed change will receive the strongest resistance and who the staunchest resisters will be. That prepares me for the next step in the process.

Step 2: Listen and Respond to Resisters

Innovators and leaders can look upon those who are resistant to their ideas as adversaries. Usually it's a case of mistaken identity.

Rather than view them as enemies to be overcome, I prefer to see them as advisers, necessary in transforming a good idea into a great idea. Their resistance is useful. Like pain in the body, it lets me know something is out of adjustment.

By listening to resisters I learn where a change is most likely to go wrong. Resisters have an uncanny ability to point out all the potential flaws within a proposal. They are superb at finding the weaknesses and hidden defects within a plan. After all, they are motivated!

When we decided a few years ago to make home fellowships the axis of our ministry, we were launching into what were, for us, relatively uncharted waters. Though the fellowships were an excellent concept, there were many bugs to be worked out. The resisters helped us find them. Because they didn't like the plan in the first place, they were quick to point out a host of potential hazards.

They feared being stuck in geographical groupings where they would share little in common except neighborhood. They worried about studies that would be no more than a sharing of ignorance, fretted over sharing exercises that were too threatening, and rebelled against the idea of highly restrictive group covenants or contracts. In short, they set an agenda of things for us to work on.

Truth be known, listening and responding to their concerns didn't win everyone over. Some folks still dug in their heels. But listening and responding did help us put together a better, more acceptable home fellowship program.

Resisters are also great at pointing out hidden psychological barriers that have to be overcome before a change can take place. Just because something is a good idea is no guarantee that people will buy it. For instance, when microwave ovens first came out, their sales were limited because people weren't using them to cook meat. The problem wasn't technological; it was psychological. Most people considered meat inadequately cooked if it lacked the familiar brown color on the outside. By listening to resisters (those who weren't buying the new ovens), the manufacturers were able to identify and remove this psychological barrier. They put browning elements in the ovens. Bingo! Sales increased dramatically.

When I'm trying to sell a change, I need to know the psychological barriers so I can tailor my presentation to overcome them. I realize that some pastors resist selling an idea, but I accept it as a necessary part of being a leader. If I am convinced that God wants a change made, or that a new program will bring great spiritual benefit to our people, then I have no qualms about trying to sell the idea. And if some "browning elements" are needed, so be it.

To identify psychological barriers, I ask myself two questions:

1. Are the resisters objecting to the proposal or the presenter? Pious-sounding objections can be used to cover up the real source of resistance: lack of trust in the one making the proposal. Newly arrived pastors often face this, particularly when the church has a history of short pastorates. The same goes for pastors feuding with their board or a particular member. Resistance to their suggestions usually centers more on them than on the proposal itself.

In that case, it is a waste of time to discuss the issues. Instead, it's time to focus on building trust and restoring relationships, or finding someone else to champion the idea.

2. Are the resisters objecting to the proposal or to the way it was presented? I find the most common presentation problem is the use of offensive language — not swear words, but loaded terms and phrases that carry a negative connotation to the listeners. While serving as an assistant pastor, I suggested an internship program to disciple people planning to go into full-time ministry. Since our church was near a seminary and a couple of Christian schools, I figured the idea would go over big. It didn't. The board rejected it without discussion.

When I sought to understand the reasons for their opposition, I discovered my predecessor had been fired for focusing his ministry on a small group of "disciples" at the expense of everyone else. As a result, words like *intern* and *discipleship* conjured up images of favoritism. By using these terms in my proposal, I had unwittingly torpedoed my idea. The board wasn't against training people for future ministry; they opposed the abuses of the past.

So I reframed the proposal as a Vocational Ministry Training Program, spelled out some time limitations, and left the rest of the program virtually untouched. Within a month, I had not only my program (by unanimous consent); I had twice the funding I'd requested.

I find that listening and responding to resisters is a vital step in the change process. Not that I grant every critic veto power over potential changes. But I assume my critics are, for the most part, honest and intelligent people who are concerned with different issues and problems. By carefully listening to their objections, I invariably end up with a much better idea or program.

Step 3: Sell Individuals before Groups

The need to sell individuals before trying to sell the entire group is one of the most neglected rules of group persuasion. Years ago I saw a painful illustration of what happens when this principle is ignored. A long-range-planning committee, after nearly two years of work, held a special congregational meeting to review their findings and proposals. The presentation was beautifully done, and their proposals were excellent.

But the congregation rejected their plans outright. The pastor and committee members were devastated. They had assumed a clear presentation of an excellent idea would result in congregational approval. They were wrong.

By presenting the proposal to the entire church first, the planning committee forced people to go public with their initial reactions. This practically guaranteed rejection, for two reasons. First, initial responses to change are often negative. Second, a public response is usually permanent. When an idea is presented to an entire group, everyone's opinion becomes a matter of public record, and public stands are hard to change. While people often talk themselves into an idea they initially rejected, they seldom do that once they've gone public with their opinion. That's why selling individuals first is so important: It makes it much easier for people to change their minds.

Another reason for first selling individuals is that most people won't adopt a new idea until they see that others have bought in. Those who study the process of change point out that only about 15 percent of us will adopt a new idea without first knowing who else is supporting it.

The long-range-planning committee assumed the only relevant question was "Is this a good idea?" They failed to realize that most folks also wanted to know, "Who else is for it?" When they couldn't point to anyone but themselves, people considered the idea suspect. Selling some individuals before the meeting would have given their ideas credibility.

I've tried to sell individuals every time we've needed to add a new staff position. Before presenting the proposal to the congregation, I make sure the staff, the board, and ten to twenty other people are solidly behind the idea. And when possible, we've set up a starter fund to help pay for the new position. That lets everyone know the idea has broad support, enough to have raised a few thousand dollars.

But even when all these steps have been followed, don't expect all resistance to melt away. The fact is, some people will be against every change — the sort of folks who would vote against the Second Coming if given a chance.

When faced with their opposition, I move into the last phase of the change process.

Step 4: Lead Boldly

By leading boldly, I don't mean running roughshod over those who disagree with me. I do mean stepping forward to champion a cause: clearly making my views known and doing everything I can to persuade the holdouts to follow.

For many of us, this type of leadership doesn't come easily. It runs counter to our image of a pastor as gentle shepherd. It forces people to act or react. And at times, it means offending a dear saint or long-time supporter, or even losing a key family.

Yet sometimes bold leadership is needed or inertia will rule. The fear of upsetting a few can allow a handful of critics to hold off an army of supporters. We can end up with a ministry that resembles a bus with one accelerator and sixty sets of brakes.

Just how bold to be depends on a variety of factors. First, there is the issue of God's will. The clearer I sense his leading, the bolder I am willing to be. But few changes are black and white. Only a few times in fifteen years of ministry have I pulled out the heavy artillery and publicly stated, "I'm positive God wants us to do this."

A second consideration is the price I will have to pay for boldly championing the cause. Determining that is the purpose of testing the waters. If the change is going to be too costly, bold leadership isn't a sign of valor; it's a sign of stupidity.

A third question I ask myself is, *Whom will we lose?* Notice, I don't ask *if* we will lose some people, but *which ones.* No ministry can keep everybody happy. Losing some folks to the church down the street is unavoidable. The only question is, Who will they be?

When our board and I made a commitment to contemporary worship music a few years ago, it didn't set well with a few old-timers. But prior to the change, we were losing a lot of visitors who didn't relate to traditional hymns. Many of these folks were outstanding Christians, the type of people we needed if we were going to expand our ministry. Even more significant, we weren't keeping many of the new Christians and non-Christians we were targeting.

There came a time when we had to ask, "Whom do we want to lose?" We decided we didn't want to keep losing the people we were losing. So we championed the change, and sure enough, we lost a few old-time families. But each time one family left, they were quickly replaced by three or four new ones who were looking for what we now had.

The final question I ask before pushing for a major change is, "How long do I plan to be around after the change is made?" If the answer is, "Not long," I don't push for the change.

A friend accepted a call to a small, struggling, suburban church a few years ago. While the church had potential, it wasn't going to go anywhere without major changes. He began to make those: He altered the service, changed the constitution, and adapted the facility. Though difficult, and costly in the loss of a few families, the changes allowed the church to begin to grow finally.

The only problem was that he didn't stay long enough to firmly establish the changes. Not long after they were made, he left. When he returned to visit just two years after leaving, he was disappointed to find most of his changes had been reversed. The service, atmosphere, and low attendance were strikingly similar to what he had encountered when he first came.

Leading boldly requires staying. Change is always difficult, no matter how great the gains might be. Why send a body through loss of equilibrium if we aren't going to be around to help it regain balance? Why risk driving away key old-timers if we aren't going to remain to help the new folks gain a sense of ownership?

During the past nine years, our church has taken a new name, moved to a different location, shifted our program emphasis, changed board structure, and altered worship style. Yet these changes have been accomplished largely without conflicts and deviant behavior.

I remember when we went so far as to replace our Sunday evening service with home Bible studies. Not long after we dropped the evening service, a young father came to me.

"I grew up in a church where every change was a major battle," he said. "So when I heard what you and the board were proposing, I was worried. My wife and I even thought of leaving before the battle broke out. We couldn't believe it when nothing happened. I still can't believe how easily people accepted the change."

It was not nearly as easy as it looked. But I was glad he saw it that way.

ELEVEN

CREATING SUCCESSFUL PERFORMANCE REVIEWS

A performance review can be one of the most delicate and risky parts of the pastor-board relationship. Despite the potential dangers, though, the hazards of avoiding a careful review are even greater.

Most pastors I know are deeply committed to personal growth. Not many are willing to settle for mediocrity. The vast majority spend hours reading, praying, and studying in an unending quest for spiritual and professional growth.

Yet, curiously, many of us avoid perhaps the most vital ingredient for growth — someone to candidly tell us how we are doing.

My friend Dave, in fifteen years of ministry, has never received a formal evaluation. It's not that he is unaware of the potential benefits. It's just that he is keenly aware of the potential pitfalls. He knows firsthand the sting of betrayal. There's no way he's going to give a small group of adversaries an open forum for airing grievances. As far as he is concerned, the potential dangers of a review far outweigh possible benefits.

In many ways, Dave is right. Opening ourselves to review is risky. Expecting the precise scalpel of correction, we can get the blunt ax of criticism. I know two pastors who left seemingly successful ministries within months of a bungled evaluation. There is no question: a performance review can be one of the most delicate and risky parts of the pastor-board relationship.

Despite the potential dangers, though, the hazards of avoiding a careful review are even greater.

Why Risk It?

We all have a natural tendency to exaggerate our strengths and downplay our weaknesses. One study of more than 800,000 people found that everyone in the test sample rated himself above average in the "ability to get along with others." Only 2 percent saw themselves as below average in "leadership ability." Obviously, at least half the folks were mistaken. Someone needed to help them sort reality from wishful thinking.

The fact is, we all have spiritual and personal blind spots. Just as with a loose thread or twisted collar, we seldom know they're there until someone dares to speak up.

If left alone, my blind spots become hardened personality traits. In the spiritual realm, they can become "high places," areas of overlooked sin, similar to the high places of evil sacrifice that even the best of Judah's kings ignored. I don't want that to happen, so that means asking people to tell me how I'm doing.

Still, I'm hesitant to open myself for examination until I'm reasonably sure I can get the feedback I need without getting ambushed. That's why I've developed some guidelines for my pastoral reviews.

Initiate the Process

Perhaps the most effective way to eliminate potential problems is to make sure I am the one who initiates the process. This offers several benefits.

1. A self-initiated review disarms most potential enemies. Somehow an evaluation I've requested is radically different from one imposed by others. Critics often become friends when they perceive themselves as advisers. No longer do they feel the need to overstate every concern in order to be heard. They relax once they realize I actually want to hear what they have to say.

2. A self-initiated review allows me a measure of control over the participants. The fact is, many reviews go awry because the wrong people do the evaluating.

That was Dave's major concern. His deacon board was a mess. Two of his biggest antagonists were members; and most of the rest of the board gave little evidence of spiritual maturity or insight. As far as he was concerned, they had nothing to offer him in the realms of spiritual or personal advice.

I would agree. But Dave failed to see it wasn't necessary for his board members to do the reviewing. By initiating the process, he could choose anyone.

While serving as a youth pastor in one church, I felt the deacons, while fine people, simply didn't know me or my ministry well enough to be of much help. So I contacted some individuals involved in my area of ministry, as well as two staff pastors with whom I worked closely. I asked them to complete a brief questionnaire and then to discuss with me areas where they felt I needed to grow. To keep the deacon board from feeling slighted, I was careful to present this as a request for personal evaluation, rather than a job performance review (a prerogative that was rightly the board's).

The result? A helpful evaluation by people who knew me and my ministry well enough to move beyond superficial impressions. More important, I had no excuse to ignore their advice; after all, I had handpicked the participants.

Here at North Coast, I've been blessed with wise and godly elders, so I've used them as the primary reviewers of my life and ministry. Yet, it's important to note that I've not relinquished control or institutionalized the process. My annual evaluation remains at my pleasure. The board doesn't schedule it. I do.

If our board should ever suffer a fate similar to Dave's, I'd be able to avoid being led as a lamb to the slaughter. I would simply hold off scheduling the event and instead quietly seek out another group of advisers whose insight and spirituality I could respect.

Obviously, there is great potential for abuse here. Like Rehoboam, I can surround myself with yes men rather than wise counselors. To avoid this, I've made a commitment never to change advisers because of what they say or think, but only when their spiritual or moral failure has rendered their insight suspect.

3. A self-initiated review allows me a measure of control over the process. When a pastoral evaluation is controlled by the board or becomes institutionalized, I'm left with little say about the process. Since most lay leaders live in the business world, they tend to base pastoral appraisals and performance reviews on the models used there. I heard of one pastor whose evaluation was based on questions used by a large interstate trucking firm!

I don't want my reviews to be limited to the things covered by the typical employee review — how well I'm doing my job and how well I'm fitting into the organization's culture. I also want to know where I need to grow as a leader, father, husband, and spiritual example.

4. A self-initiated review helps me overcome the biggest obstacle to personal growth: my defensiveness. When I feel threatened, it's hard to hear what others are saying. I'm more apt to offer an excuse than change. But when I ask for a critique, instead of feeling attacked, I feel assisted. Instead of being cast in the role of an employee wondering if the bosses are happy, I'm put in the position of a leader soliciting candid advice. The difference is significant.

I consider this so important that I've never forced a formal evaluation on staff members. While we do have job descriptions and annual reviews, they fall far short of the no-holds-barred evaluation of both professional and personal life I'm talking about. I know the staff will benefit most from a review when they feel least threatened, so I let them pick the participants, process, and areas of focus — and even whether to have a review.

Choose the Time Carefully

I've also found it important to avoid being reviewed during times of great personal failure or stress. At times like these, asking the board to put our ministry and life under a microscope can be counterproductive. We already have enough stuff to work on. The last thing we need is the exposure of a few more blind spots.

My first two years at North Coast were difficult, to say the least. A change from the founding pastor's style of leadership, my own mistakes, and a poorly equipped board resulted in constant turnover. Old families seemed to leave as fast as new ones came in. Make that a little faster.

I felt I was failing miserably. Most of my peers would have agreed. I didn't need anyone to point out new areas demanding work. Based on the problems I could see and the informal feedback I was getting, I had plenty of things to work on. Right then, a formal review and airing of problems would have pushed me over the edge. I think I would have given up and tried another career. So I didn't initiate a review during those two years. Only when the church had begun to turn around did I ask for one.

That is not to say I don't seek feedback during difficult times. I get all I can. But I don't ask for a thorough critique of my life and ministry when I'm standing on the brink. Why invite someone to push me over?

I know a pastor who built a small rural church into one of the largest churches in his denomination. For twenty-four years he had enjoyed a great ministry. Then, during a personal low time, his board chose to review his administrative skills and conflict management style. The board members were not too complimentary, though they loved him and would have overlooked his weaknesses for another twenty-four years.

But because of his emotional state at the time, he was devastated. Feeling unappreciated and angry, he resigned within two weeks.

Both he and his board would have been better served if he had asked for a delay in the process. But since the evaluation was at the board's initiative, not his, he felt trapped and unable to do that. Even so, it would have been worth a try. Things hardly could have ended up worse.

Obviously, if I find myself continually facing failure and great stress, something is wrong. In that case, I probably need candid feedback to find out what I'm doing to help cause the situation. But if the failure or stress is an isolated incident, I stay away from the high-intensity searchlight. I already have enough things to work on.

Avoid Anonymous Responses

Many people assume that anonymity increases candor. I have my doubts. But one thing I know for sure: anonymous responses undermine an effective pastoral review.

First, anonymous responses ignore a basic principle of evaluation: Criticisms and compliments should be weighed, not counted.

A few years ago, one of our most strait-laced board members complained I was a bit too earthy. I shrugged it off. By his standards, I wanted to be. But when another, tough-skinned individual pointed out how I had hurt his feelings, I set about immediately to see that it wouldn't happen again.

The fact is, Dave will always want more of an evangelistic emphasis, while Jim will want greater depth. Pete will think I am refreshingly candid; Don will label me as too blunt. Only by knowing *who* said what can I tell the significance of an observation.

A second problem with anonymity is that it often fosters misunderstanding. By its nature, an anonymous response makes clarification and explanation impossible.

During one annual review, I received an evaluation that said I was a loner and unsupportive of others. I was shocked and hurt. That was one complaint I'd never heard; I couldn't figure it out. Fortunately, since the evaluations were signed, I was able to ask the individual what he meant. He told me he was concerned that I was not involved with, or supportive of, our denomination. In no way, he said, did he mean I was a loner or unsupportive of the people in the church. He just wanted to see me more involved in the larger church family.

When I explained that I attended without fail a voluntary monthly meeting with our district superintendent, and that I was also serving on a district ordination committee, he was satisfied. Because I rarely spoke of these things, he had assumed I didn't support the denomination. Had his critique been anonymous, I would have worried that I was being perceived as out of touch with our people, and he would have continued to be irritated with my seeming lack of support for the larger body of Christ.

Perhaps the most common and dangerous form of an anonymous review is the one carried out in the pastor's absence. According to the typical scenario, a group evaluates the pastor's life or ministry and then sends one member to communicate the results. This makes clarification nearly impossible. It forces the pastor to rely on one person's interpretation of what was said, meant, and felt by the others. Even worse, it gives an antagonist an opportunity to make unchallenged accusations. Usually, by the time these are cleared up, damage has already been done.

I've become quite hard-nosed about anonymous advice or criticism. Unsigned letters and notes go unread to the trash. People who won't say something to my face have no right to be heard. If I can't get an honest answer without anonymity, I'm left with serious questions about a person's integrity and courage. And if, on the other hand, people are so intimidated by my presence that they can't respond openly, I have bigger problems than any pastoral review will be able to solve.

Get It In Writing

Still another pitfall I've learned to avoid is the verbal review in which people offer appraisals without first having written them. Why get observations in writing?

First, many people have a hard time expressing negative or critical opinions face to face. Others feel insecure thinking on their feet. To ask for a candid verbal review is unfair to them; they simply can't give one. Yet many of these same people have no problem when asked to put their thoughts on paper. Somehow, writing frees them to say things they never would dare say aloud. Their answers become more detailed and straightforward. At the same time, asking for written responses has never inhibited our more verbal members. They simply jot a brief answer and expand on it when their turn to speak comes.

A second reason for insisting on written evaluations is that they can't be swayed by the consensus of the meeting. Verbal responses are easily swayed by the remarks of those who speak first.

So during my annual review I ask each participant to write his observations (sometimes ahead of time). I either collect the papers or go around the room and have people read them. Only after all comments are on the table do we discuss them. This way, I'm exposed to people's original thoughts and feelings, and the more articulate and verbal members have a harder time dominating the group.

Change Evaluation Tools Often

Another way to maximize the benefit of a pastoral review is to change evaluation tools frequently. Questions, no matter how good or insightful, soon become routine. Only once have I used the same tool two years in a row. I did it because the first time went so well. But the second time, people's answers were short and superficial. One man asked, "Why do we need to keep harping on this stuff?"

Using the same evaluation tool a second time does have one advantage. It allows you to measure growth from one year to the next. But I've found there is usually enough overlap among tools to still give me a good idea of progress.

By using a variety of questionnaires and formats, I've been able to get feedback in many areas and from different perspectives. Last year's review focused on my life in general. The year before we zeroed in on ministry skills. Others have focused on my preaching, leadership style, or spiritual walk. By looking at myself from each of these perspectives, I've been able to get a more accurate reading of my strengths and weaknesses.

Evaluation tools can be found in a variety of places. I've found some in books, such as Gene Getz's *The Measure of a Man*. Others were found in old issues of LEADERSHIP or adapted from professional and devotional magazines. Still others have come via friends in other denominational settings. And the "Tests and Measurements" section of a local library is a gold mine of instruments that have been designed and used in psychological and management research.

Avoid Combining Performance and Salary Reviews

Finally, it's important to keep a pastoral review separate from salary reviews. Not that a salary shouldn't be tied to performance (Scriptures like 1 Timothy 5:17–18 suggest they're related), but I will not be as open to personal growth during a review tied to salary considerations as I will during one that's entirely separate. Frankly, if the results of my review affect my salary, I won't be too eager for people to bring up areas needing work. Yet sadly, the most common time for pastors to receive an evaluation is during their annual salary review.

I like to schedule my annual review after our budget is set. As I see it, a pastoral review and a salary review have two different purposes. A salary review is to determine a fair and equitable salary in light of responsibilities, skills, and experience. A pastoral review is to help me to discover more accurately what I do well and what I need to work on. One sets my compensation level; the other determines my personal agenda.

If a review must be tied to salary considerations, I would schedule it three to six months before salaries are determined. This way there is time to work on areas needing improvement before final decisions are made. Otherwise, those who receive a negative evaluation are stuck for the next year with a monthly reminder of the previous year's problems. Rather than motivate growth, this is likely to arouse resentment and a change of address. Even worse is an excellent review followed by a meager pay increase. Most people quickly forget the positive words when they're followed by a paltry paycheck.

Faithful Wounds

By carefully following these guidelines, I've been able to make my annual review something I actually look forward to. It's the one time I can take stock of where I've been and where I need to go. At my first review at North Coast, while I heard plenty of praise, there were also some harsh criticisms. In particular, we discussed my insensitivity to people who see things differently. I also discovered I wasn't delegating nearly as effectively as I had thought.

Later that night, our board chairman called. He sounded worried. "Are you doing okay, Larry?" he asked. "I was afraid you might have been crushed by some of the things we said." Actually, I'd rushed home to tell my wife what a fantastic meeting it had been. My board had been open with me. I had learned a great deal about myself and my ministry.

What our chairman failed to grasp was that, in the controlled environment of my pastoral review, I had not been unfairly criticized. I had received the faithful wounds of my friends. There is no comparison between the two.

TWELVE

NEGOTIATING A FAIR SALARY

When good people get the facts straight, the outcome is usually fair for all concerned.

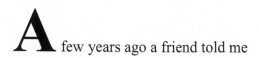 few years ago a friend told me how he had felt compelled to leave a growing Midwest church after a series of below-inflation pay raises. With three teenage children, he found himself unable to keep up with the rising costs of raising a family.

For years, he had swallowed hard and hoped things would be different next year. They never were. Feeling discouraged and unappreciated, he accepted a call to another church.

Tragically, the church he left had been happy with his ministry. As far as they were concerned, everything was going well. They had no idea he was unhappy and didn't want him to leave. But by then it was too late. Not wanting to repeat the mistake, they hired their next pastor at a substantially higher salary, a salary that would have been more than enough to meet my friend's needs.

He still might be pastoring that church if only he had known how to negotiate a fair salary. Instead, the church lost a pastor it wanted to keep; he lost a ministry he loved.

Admittedly, my friend's case is an extreme example, but his problem is not isolated. While many pastors have been well trained in the theological and pastoral realms, few receive any instruction in hammering out a reasonable pay package.

I, too, had to learn the hard way. When I arrived at my first pastorate, I discovered one man held the offices of board chairman, finance elder, and treasurer. He was also the driving force behind our fledgling building program. His number one priority was to save enough money to purchase property for us to build on. As a result, my "promotion" from youth pastor to a senior position resulted in a three-thousand-dollar cut in pay and benefits. I figured I'd better learn to negotiate. If I didn't, I might soon be paying for the privilege of pastoring a church!

Over the years things have changed. The congregation has been more than generous, and I have no financial complaints. Much of the credit belongs to a kind and supportive board, but some belongs to the principles of negotiation I have learned along the way.

My concept of negotiation is simple. I have just two major goals: (1) to produce a fair salary, and (2) to avoid any hint of an adversarial relationship with the board. Here are the principles that have helped me reach those goals.

Commitment to Openness and Honesty

Fair negotiations are founded on a commitment to openness and honesty. Since most of us strive to develop more open and honest relationships with our congregations, this shouldn't be a problem. But our commitment to openness and honesty often gets sabotaged at salary time, undercut by an equally strong hesitancy to talk about money.

I know that in my role as pastor, I hate talking about money. I cringe at the thought of a building or fund-raising program. It bothers me when record numbers of visitors show up on Stewardship Sunday. There lies the problem. At negotiation time, my hesitancy to talk about money conflicts with my desire for openness and honesty.

Many of us let our distaste for discussing money win out; we keep our feelings inside. We say "Thank you" when we really mean "That's not enough!" The result is often an unfair salary and a dissatisfied pastor.

Whenever I hear a pastor friend complain about some aspect of his contract, I listen, and then I casually ask if he has told his board members or the salary review committee how he feels.

Invariably, the answer is no.

When I ask why, I am given a variety of reasons, but the bottom line is usually fear. Some pastors fear getting their heads bitten off; others fear the appearance of greed or a lack of contentment. Some fear breaking the spiritual relationship with their board.

But the truth is, most pastors have nothing to fear. While it's true that some boards are out to "keep the pastor humble," most are made up of good people who want nothing more than to faithfully serve God and support their pastor. There is no need to fear being open and honest with such people.

As we talked one day, Gary, a fellow pastor, expressed discouragement with the level of recent raises. After seven years of solid ministry, he felt he wasn't being adequately compensated. I asked if he had ever told any of his board members how he felt.

As usual, the answer was no. So I challenged him to tell even one or two of his board members what he had told me. I knew he was doing a fine job and that his board was pleased with his ministry. I figured they simply had no idea how he felt.

I was right. The next time I saw Gary, he informed me that his board had not only listened to his request; they had responded with a significant increase.

When we complain to outsiders and friends before we have expressed those same feelings to the board, we are being less than forthright. We're ignoring the "golden rule" — failing to treat the board the same way we want our parishioners to treat us when they are upset by our actions or decisions.

A caution: It's important to know who can handle honest feelings. Openness and honesty does not mean foolishly giving ammunition to those who would hurt us. When faced with a divided board or a one-man thorn in the flesh, it is usually best to start by sharing your feelings with more loyal supporters on the board.

However, to be effective, we can't limit transparency to our best friends. We have to talk to those who will actually make the decision. In marketing, it's called "selling the decision maker." In other words, when you're selling hand organs, don't talk to the monkey.

It's unfortunate that so many pastors are leery of honesty when it comes to their compensation package, for without an open and honest exchange, pastor and board are left with assumptions and guesswork, a wholly inadequate basis for decision making.

Time for Reflection and Feedback

The second key principle is to build into the salary review process adequate time for reflection and feedback.

Obviously, the best time for feedback comes before, not after, the board has finalized next year's salary. Yet most pastors have no opportunity to review their proposed package before it is finalized. Instead, it's set in a frustratingly arbitrary manner, without any opportunity for their input.

Often a weary board decides next year's salary at the end of a late-night budget meeting. After the pastor or pastors have been asked to leave the room, the treasurer suggests a salary figure he feels the budget can handle. A brief discussion follows; then the board adopts a figure remarkably close to the treasurer's proposal.

No wonder many pastors feel frustrated with such a process. It wouldn't be so bad if a well-rested group carefully evaluated the implications of the proposal for both the church and the pastor. But it hurts to watch your family's financial security rise and fall with the whims of an exhausted board.

Wanting to put an end to such scenarios, I requested that we add a "week of reflection" to our annual review process. It is not a week for hardball negotiations but simply an opportunity for my staff and me to reflect upon the proposed changes in our contract and how they will affect us during the coming year.

I asked the board to give me this week to think and pray over their proposed compensation package before it was finalized. I promised honest feedback at the end of the week. I also assured them I would willingly accept their decision to adopt or reject any changes I might propose. I just wanted them to know how I felt before they made their final decision.

This week of reflection has proved to have two major benefits for our church and staff. First, it has given us a forum for discussing and correcting inequities brought about by false assumptions or misunderstanding. We can clarify issues the board might not be fully aware of: the impact of rising social security taxes and inflation, or the added cost of feeding teenagers. This week also allows us to correct inadvertent mistakes. One year our elder board decided to completely rework my compensation package. In the process, they thought they were giving me a substantial raise. So did I. When I took a sharp pencil to the figures, however, I realized the actual result of the changes would be a cut in monthly income. Given the complicated nature of the changes, without a week of reflection I would not have realized their implications until after the package had been finalized. My "raise" would have been lost, and worse, I would have had no forum from which to ask the board to reconsider.

A second benefit of our week of reflection has been the opportunity to vent frustrations and feelings before they become major issues. For instance, my annual vacation allotment aggravated me for a long time. It was a purely symbolic issue, but the type that can easily be blown out of proportion. In my previous ministry, I had earned four weeks of annual vacation. When I was called to North Coast, they offered two weeks. We settled on three.

Thanks to our week of reflection, I had a vehicle to voice my complaint to the board, rather than to outsiders. Each year I carefully explained why I felt the vacation time should be expanded. Each year they returned to tell me they thought it was ample. Yet there was something amazingly cathartic about the process. Even when they said no, somehow the tension and frustration were removed. I no longer felt I was on the receiving end of uninformed and arbitrary decisions. I knew they understood how I felt, so it was okay if they disagreed with me.

And after five years, I got my four weeks. But, in the interim, I had a vehicle to vent my honest feelings and keep this admittedly minor and symbolic issue from growing into a major source of hurt or frustration.

We've found the week of reflection to be the proverbial ounce of prevention worth a pound of cure.

Comparison of Apples with Apples

A third principle in negotiating a fair salary is to be sure everyone is comparing apples with apples. Many unfair compensation packages are the result of not knowing how to compare accurately a pastor's salary with a layperson's salary.

Most board members have no idea of the true cost of their salary. When you ask the average layperson what he makes, he is likely to give you an amount equal to his take-home pay or, if he is salaried, his gross salary. He will almost never include the cost to his employer for such items as medical insurance, employer contributions to social security, retirement, or other benefits. My friends in business say these expenses usually add at least 40 percent to the gross salary. In other words, a man who thinks his salary is thirty thousand dollars a year, in actuality will be making something closer to forty-two thousand dollars. And this figure will be higher if the job has especially good benefits.

Yet when a church looks at its pastor's salary, it often looks not at the cash salary of the pastor but at the cost to the church of providing a pastor. People then figure the pastor is making thousands of dollars more than he or she actually makes, and compared to their pay stubs, the pastor's compensation appears out of line.

To help my board and congregation to more accurately compare salaries, I suggested we reorganize our budget categories. Our budget originally had a category entitled *Pastor*, which included my salary, housing allowance, and medical insurance. It also included many items that should not have been confused with salary: mileage and entertainment reimbursements, professional dues and subscriptions, the cost of attending denominational conferences, continuing education expenses, and book allowances. These represent the cost of running a ministry. They should no more be confused with the pastor's salary than should the cost of having a secretary or lighting the office. If the money is mine to spend as I please, it's salary. If it is a reimbursement for the cost of work I am expected to do, or meetings I am expected to attend, it's an administrative expense.

To reflect this, we put all these expenses of running a ministry into a category called *Administration*, the same one that contained the utilities, postage, office supplies, and insurance. Now when the board and the congregation look at the salary figures, they can more accurately compare them with their own.

Even with these changes, there are still areas where a pastor's salary cannot be compared exactly with a layperson's. For instance, few lay people (except military personnel) have a tax-exempt housing allowance. Not many lay people understand how it works. Some underestimate its benefits; others vastly exaggerate its worth.

Often lay people also misunderstand self-employment taxes. Since most pastors are self-employed for social security purposes, they pay a substantially higher social security tax than those who work as company employees. Unless a lay person is self-employed, half of his social security taxes are paid by his employer. It's another part of that extra 40 percent most people forget about when figuring their salary. Those who make the final salary decisions need to understand these differences and their implications.

The purpose of structuring an annual budget in this way is not to trick anybody, nor to make a raise easier to come by. It's simply to insure that people are comparing apples with apples when they review the pastor's annual salary.

An Established Standard

The final principle I'll mention is to agree upon a standard by which pastoral salaries will be set. Some denominations set these, but if not, the board's standard will usually be only "What can we afford?" While that is an important question, it should not be the only one.

Setting objective standards is particularly important when the makeup of the board or finance committee changes from year to year. Without some benchmarks, the criteria change every time a new committee meets.

To build stability into our system, our board asks three questions when setting staff salaries:

1. What would it cost to replace this person with someone of equal skills and abilities? That's important, because if we are significantly underpaying a person, chances are, they won't be with us too long.

To answer the question, all we have to do is ask ourselves, Whom would we try to hire if this staff member left? Then we try to ascertain their current salary and benefits.

Assuming we want to keep the staff person, it's shortsighted to pay less than their replacement would cost. Any owner of a company knows that employee turnover is fraught with hidden costs: moving expenses, training, lost productivity. In the church, an area of ministry almost always suffers a significant loss of momentum when its leader leaves. And quickly hiring a replacement is no guarantee things will soon be back to normal. Paying the going rate is a small price for stability.

In the case of a staff member who's doing a bang-up job, I encourage our board to go one step further and slap on "golden handcuffs." By paying a little more than the going rate, the board sends a strong message of affirmation and insures the person won't leave just because someone comes along with a better offer.

2. What secular jobs parallel this position in responsibility and the education and skills needed for success? Though this question is somewhat subjective — two groups could come up with different parallel jobs — it helps avoid gross inequities.

In asking this question it's important to avoid superficial answers. A friend served in a newly planted church where the board decided his job paralleled a school teacher's. So they called the school board to find out what a second-year teacher made. Unfortunately, they failed to factor in educational credits and the fact that a school teacher's contract covers only the school year. What they thought was a comparable situation in reality had little in common.

It's also best to ask this question annually, for as a church grows, the parallels change. Some youth pastors have a job comparable to a camp counselor's; others are in a situation approximating a high school teacher's. Pastors' situations may resemble a school teacher's, a principal's, or a company president's.

3. What can we afford? Because church budgets are notoriously tight, this question needs to be asked last, not first. Those who start with it will almost always end up with the same answer: "Not much."

My friend Steve took a position as assistant pastor in a small Baptist church. His starting pay was deplorable, but it was all the church could afford, so he accepted it gladly. As the church grew, so did the annual budget. But the need for new programs, expanded facilities, and additional staff always ate up the increase. There was never enough money left over to bring Steve's salary up to par. Unable to catch up, Steve quit four years later. Only then did the board ask what the position was worth, and they were shocked when they found out what it would cost to replace him.

Like Steve and me, most of our staff members have joined at a salary below the going rate. At the time, it was all the church could afford. But unlike Steve, they've not been stuck there, even though our budget is generally as tight as everyone else's.

The reason? Our board sets a standard; they ask what they *should* pay before asking what they *can* pay. So when the church grows and giving goes up, it's already decided what we will do with some of the additional money. We'll try to improve salaries. A couple of times that has resulted in large raises within months of a staff member's arrival. The raises never would have happened if the board hadn't first set a standard for what the position was worth.

An unfair salary is a costly mistake, not only for the pastor, but also for the church. It breeds disillusionment, frustration, and turnover. That's why it's important for the pastor to be more than a passive participant in the salary decisions.

Fortunately, negotiating a fair salary is not a matter of playing hardball. It's simply a matter of communicating, making sure people get the facts they need in order to make an informed decision. For when good people get the facts straight, the outcome is usually fair for all concerned.

THIRTEEN

WHAT GAME ARE WE PLAYING?

Ministry growth is more than adding players, sometimes it's a whole new ball game.

Something stirred inside me the first time I heard Ben describe the church he was planting. I didn't know whether it was awe or jealousy. He had all the bases covered. From philosophy of ministry to vision and goals, he knew where he was headed and how he was going to get there.

He had mapped out a clear and powerful system of discipleship, church governance, leadership structures and ministry patterns. I was sure that he was laying down a solid foundation upon which to build his ministry. So was he.

Now, years later, we both realize he was actually making a critical mistake. His clearly laid out plans and structures were inadvertently producing an organizational straight jacket that would constrict and choke off the very entrepreneurial spirit that initially caused his church to boom.

What happened?

Ben failed to realize that *growth changes everything*. With structures and patterns so strongly stated and so firmly entrenched, he made it nearly impossible to change them when they no longer worked. And since his leadership molds couldn't be broken, it was the church that eventually broke.

Like Ben, many church leaders fail to understand that more members and staff don't just make a church bigger. They make it different. Roles and relationships change, often dramatically, and usually unintentionally. And if these changes are either unrecognized or unwanted, it's not long until conflict erupts.

Over the years, the church that I pastor, North Coast Church, has slowly and steadily grown. More like a glacier than an avalanche, we've worked our way through the various stages of growth from a one-man show to a so-called megachurch. Along the way, we've had to reinvent our structures, roles and relationships many times. Some changes were so natural we hardly noticed them. Others were more difficult, some gut-wrenching. But all the changes were inescapable. Our only choice was to embrace them or resist them – we could not avoid them.

I liken these adaptations to the changes an athlete must go through as he or she switches from playing one sport to another. With each new season and sport, there are significant differences in roles, rules and relationships. The same holds true for your church or organization. As it grows, you can count on some predictable changes in the way the leadership team relates and functions. Here are some of the key changes you can expect at each stage.

The Track & Field Star

The role of the solo pastorate can be compared to that of a track and field star. It's a role that is particularly unique and challenging. It's where most of us start out, and many choose to stay. On the up-side it offers tremendous freedom. On the down-side, it can be overwhelming and lonely.

Like the high jumper or sprinter, the solo pastor may work out with others, but he performs alone – often, without fanfare or support, and usually before a small crowd peppered with close family and friends.

Independent types love it. Sometimes the highly relational do, too, because the smaller size of the congregation can provide an opportunity for deeper personal relationships. But often, these smaller churches (especially those with a long history of in-grown relationships) can shut out a new pastor, viewing him as an outsider to be tolerated rather than a leader to be followed.

Perhaps that's why most of the solo pastors and leaders I've known look forward to someday being a part of a team. So much so, they often end up pulling together a group of lay leaders or close friends to create a sense of teamwork and shared ministry.

Golfing Buddies

With growth, the leadership team inevitably grows. And it is the game of golf that best illustrates the dynamics of a small leadership team. Whereas the solo pastor's role and relationships parallel those of a track star, a leadership team composed of two to four key members relates more like buddies on the golf course than competitors on the track.

Golf is a highly relational game. So are these teams. Golf is most enjoyable when played with friends. And while it's preferable to have similar skills, a stroke a hole is no big deal among friends. The leisurely pace allows for extended conversation and camaraderie. In fact, it's a major part of the game. Afterward, everyone hangs around for a snack and a drink while debriefing the round and planning the next one.

For the highly relational pastor, a golf-sized staff or leadership team is often the most enjoyable stage. The relationships are often deep, the sharing genuine, and the concern for one another goes far beyond the golf course. Doing what you like with people you like is hard to beat.

The Basketball Team

More of a team sport than a friendship sport, basketball depends upon working together, trusting one another, and sharing the ball. Unlike golfing buddies, no one expects everyone on a basketball team to be best friends. There are too many players for that.

That doesn't mean that quality relationships are no longer important. It just means they are different. While basketball teams don't usually have the same depth of relationships found among golfing buddies, the good ones still have excellent *esprit de corps*. Everyone rides to the game in a large van or small bus. The locker room is small and intimate. Trash talking is half the fun.

But as the size of the leadership team grows, roles are no longer as egalitarian as they once were. Some become stars and some role players. Fact is: A winning basketball team needs a star player or two – what coaches call a "go-to-guy." Given lots of freedom to go one-on-one, these players can make or break a team. And adding or losing a star player is a big deal. It can turn the season around.

One thing that doesn't change at this stage is the players' awareness of what's going on around them. Like buddies on the golf course, members of a basketball team all know what the other players are doing and what everyone is supposed to do. During the game, those not in the game watch those who are. Everyone plays offense and defense. And when the coach addresses the team, he speaks to everyone at once.

Finally at this size, changing roles for the good of the team can usually be done without asking anyone to make too large of a personal sacrifice. Like members of a basketball team, each player on your leadership team may have a role, but most players can play multiple positions.

For many entrepreneurial leaders, the basketball stage is perhaps the most enjoyable (especially when looking back). It retains much of the relational closeness found on the golf course while adding the ego satisfaction of playing the game in a bigger arena before a much larger crowd.

The Football Team

When your leadership team or ministry staff increases to 15, 25, in some cases, 50 or more, the game changes radically. More like a football team, the dynamics of this size group can be very unsettling for those who *prefer* golf or basketball. And for those who still *think* they're playing golf or basketball, life on the football field can get downright painful.

Football is a game of highly specialized roles. Few players are inter-changeable. Guards seldom become quarterbacks. Teamwork is more important than one-on-one skill. In fact, a great athlete who insists on continually freelancing can mess up the entire offense or defense. The same holds true for a larger leadership team.

At this stage, it's no longer possible for everyone to know what everyone else is doing. Unlike their counterparts on the golf course or basketball court, football players don't know all that is going on – and they don't expect to know.

The offensive and defensive teams have different game plans and play books. When not in the game, football players don't watch the game; they huddle with their unit and position coach to plan for the next series. And most players (even most coaches) have to watch the game films to know what happened.

For the members of a leadership team that once played basketball together, this can be an especially difficult adjustment. It can leave some team members feeling insignificant, left out, no longer a vital part of the team. Some won't be able to make the change. Some won't want to. But there is nothing they can do about it. At this size, the game has changed. The only question is: Are the players going to put on the pads, retire or just stand there and get run over?

Football teams also move players around in order to put the best team on the field. But unlike basketball, switching to a new position can take some significant adjustments on the part of the player (gaining or losing weight, learning a whole new set of plays or techniques). The same holds true for staff members in a larger and more specialized leadership team. When asked to change roles for the good of the organization, the personal cost can be quite considerable.

Finally, the relationships on a football team are drastically different from those found on the golf course or a basketball court. The sheer number of players and the distinctly different roles make camaraderie a greater challenge. While a basketball team rides everywhere together, a football team must take two buses. While basketball players know everyone else's assignment, football players may not have a clue what others are doing on a given play. Even the locker rooms are different, with football's being large and seldom intimate.

Caught By Surprise

While these changes are inevitable in a growing leadership team, many leaders don't see them coming – or realize when they've already taken place. It reminds me of a fellow I played basketball with in high school.

A star football player and good athlete, Todd decided to go out for the varsity basketball team. He made the team. But whenever it came time to play hard-nosed defense, he reverted to the tactics he'd learned on the football field. He never quite understood that this was a new game with new rules.

What Todd, the football player, called, "a little pushing and shoving," the basketball referees called "a foul." Soon Todd was on the bench, confused and frustrated that the officials didn't appreciate the tight defense that had won him awards as a cornerback.

The simplest and most predictable indicator that leadership roles and relationships might need to change is the number of people on your team. But there are others. Here are three more indicators that strongly suggest the game has changed – even if no one has yet noticed.

Relational Overload

A significant increase in the time spent massaging relationships is an early sign that the game may have changed.

My preferred style of leadership is relational. I'd rather convince you than give a directive. I don't do memos (OK, I *didn't* do memos). Instead, I prefer to pass vision and direction through ad hoc meetings around lunch or the water cooler.

That worked well for a long while. Adding a weekly scheduled staff meeting was all we needed to transition from golf to basketball. At this stage, we hit our stride. We hummed along for a decade on a long, winning streak. It was a blast. Everyone was happy. We jokingly called our staff "the black hole" because when someone joined, they never left.

But with steady growth in attendance, came a constant need to add new players. Eventually, we were no longer an overgrown basketball team. We were a football team. But since people came aboard one at a time, I didn't realize that the game had changed. But I did notice that I was spending a lot of time trying to keep everyone happy and in the loop.

Slowly, I found myself sucked into a relational nightmare. Since most of the ministry team thought we were still playing basketball, they were upset any time something happened without their knowledge. Since I thought we were still playing basketball, I assumed their complaints were legitimate. So I'd spend hours each week trying to catch up with anyone who'd been left out of the loop, gone for the day, missed a meeting or in any way wanted to have input into a decision.

Time to reflect, lead and study disappeared, squeezed into the late evenings and early mornings. Days off became days to catch up. What had once been an energizing ministry became a dreaded job.

Only when I realized that I was trying to play basketball with a football team did I find my way out.

Increased Miscommunication

Another sign that the game may be changing is an increase in miscommunication. When important messages are chronically missed or misunderstood, it's time to change the way we play the game.

In the golf-sized team, communication is easy and natural; there is seldom a need to set up a special meeting to discuss anything. You're already together most of the time.

When our staff was small we hardly ever had a scheduled meeting. It felt silly to do so. If we had something to discuss, we did it on the spot. It was fun and fluid, and took little time or planning. But as our staff grew, someone was always missing, out of town or in a meeting. Our preferred style became ineffective; we needed to make our communication more structured and intentional.

I used to coach my son's youth league basketball teams. Occasionally, another team would throw a surprise defense or press our way. I quickly learned that nothing is harder than trying to explain to the kids in the middle of a game what was happening and how to beat it.

The information was not that complicated. All I needed was a chalk board, about two minutes of explanation, and a few walk-throughs. The problem was simply the number of people who needed to grasp it. If just one kid misunderstood or tuned out, we'd turn the ball over; no matter how well the others understood.

Usually, we'd just do the best we could and then deal with it at the next practice.

It's the same way with a leadership team. The larger the team and the more hectic the game, the greater the need for special meetings, chalk talks, and film sessions to keep everyone on the same page. And if the team keeps growing, you'll have to devise even more structured and intentional communication tools.

That's not as easy as it sounds. Expect resistance. Duffers who thrive on leisurely fairway talks will feel cheated when you substitute rambling conversations with scripted meetings or agendas. For many of them, it's not the game; it's the relationships that count most.

Basketball players accustomed to knowing everything about the game plan are seldom thrilled when a new structure leaves them focused on only part of the picture. After all, in most organizations, knowledge holds the key to power and prestige.

Because of this resistance (and the fact that some of us like the old game better than the new game), it can be tempting to communicate in the old ways long after they no longer work. That might keep one or two players happy, but the rest of the team will flounder.

When the team grows, the team leader has two choices: either accept and adapt to the new reality, or wait until a serious conflict solves the problem by shrinking the group back to a more comfortable size.

Conflict Over The Decision-Making Process

Whenever the decision-making process becomes paralyzed or produces inordinate conflict and power plays, it's a sign that something is structurally wrong.

Most often, it will be a set of rules and assumptions stuck in the past, appropriate for a game you are no longer playing.

Occasionally, the problem comes from making decisions too quickly. This happens when a long-time track star adds a staff member or moves to a new golf-sized ministry. Used to being his own counsel, the pastor continues to make decisions without consulting (or at times even informing) the rest of the team. This is a serious breach of golf etiquette. If continued, the other players usually start looking for another partner or place to play.

More commonly, decisions are made too slowly, bottlenecked as a result of trying to include too many people in the process.

Some years ago we added just one person to a key team. Previously, this team functioned like tightly knit golfing buddies. They made great decisions. Everyone enjoyed the process. But suddenly, things fell apart. A group that once reached consensus quickly and easily started debating every little item. Coalitions formed, relationships suffered. What were once enjoyable strategy sessions became dreaded staff meetings.

What happened? The game had changed, but the players didn't know it. The problem was not the newest member. The problem was adding one player too many without changing the rules.

Look what happens each time a new person joins the decision-making mix: With two people, you have to maintain just two lines of communication. Adding a third creates six lines of communication. A fourth, 12. A fifth, 20. Add a sixth person and you now have 30 lines of communication to monitor!

No wonder growing leadership teams find their old decision-making processes breaking down.

The basic principle: As a leadership team grows, day-to-day decisions need to be pushed out to the frontline while decisions about direction and vision need to be made by an ever narrowing group at the top.

This ensures that those who make day-to-day decisions are close enough to the action to make good decisions and those who shape vision are not bogged down by relational overload. But it's here that many leadership teams get stuck. They refuse to narrow the number of people responsible for vision and directional leadership. The results are bottlenecked decisions and combative meetings as everyone jockeys for position, power or simply the right to be heard.

The real issue is not who makes decisions. It's that the decision-making architecture remains appropriate to the game we are playing. And when it no longer fits, we must be willing to change it.

As a youth, I played a variety of sports. I certainly had a favorite. But once a season began, it didn't matter which one I liked the best (or which one came most naturally). All that mattered was my ability to adjust to the game we were currently playing. In hindsight, that was great training for leadership and ministry.

Too often, organizations and leaders know what game they want to play and keep on playing no matter what the results. But once the game has changed, it's a tough way to lead. The odds of success are about the same as Tiger Woods dropping a five foot putt with a basketball. Some things won't happen, no matter how hard we try or talented we may be.

In contrast, successful leaders and healthy organizations play the game that's in season. They accept the conditions and the rules. They discern what kind of leadership is needed and they adjust their structures, roles and relationships accordingly.

And then they play ball!

NOTES

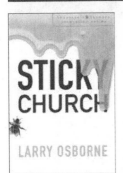

In *Sticky Church*, Larry Osborne makes the case that closing the back door of your church is far more important than opening the front door wider. He offers time-tested strategies that will practically velcro people to your ministry.

Topics include:
Why stickiness is so important
Why most discipleship models don't work very well
Why dividing groups is a dumb idea
Why people are like Legos

NORTH COAST TRAINING NETWORK
Tools & Resources for Pastors

Larry Osborne and the North Coast Training Network provide ministry resources, training events, customized workshops, and consulting for pastors and ministry teams. For a complete list or to book a customized workshop or consultation, go to www.NorthCoastChurch.com and click on Resources for Pastors and Church Leaders.

SERMON-BASED SMALL GROUP STARTER KIT: This set of DVDs features training sessions taught by Larry Osborne. Designed to get your sermon-based small groups off the ground (or to take your existing groups to new heights), each kit comes with a site license granting unlimited duplication rights for use in your church.

VIDEO VENUE STARTER KIT: This set of DVDs features conference and seminar sessions taught by Larry Osborne. Each one highlights the guiding principles and inner workings of a successful Video Venue; designed for those considering either on-site or multi-site ministry expansion. Each kit comes with unlimited duplication rights for use in your church.

21917316R10112

Made in the USA
San Bernardino, CA
11 June 2015